Aircraft of the Luftwaffe Fighter Aces I

AIRCRAFT OF THE LUFTWAFFE FIGHTER ACES I

A CHRONICLE IN PHOTOGRAPHS

Bernd Barbas

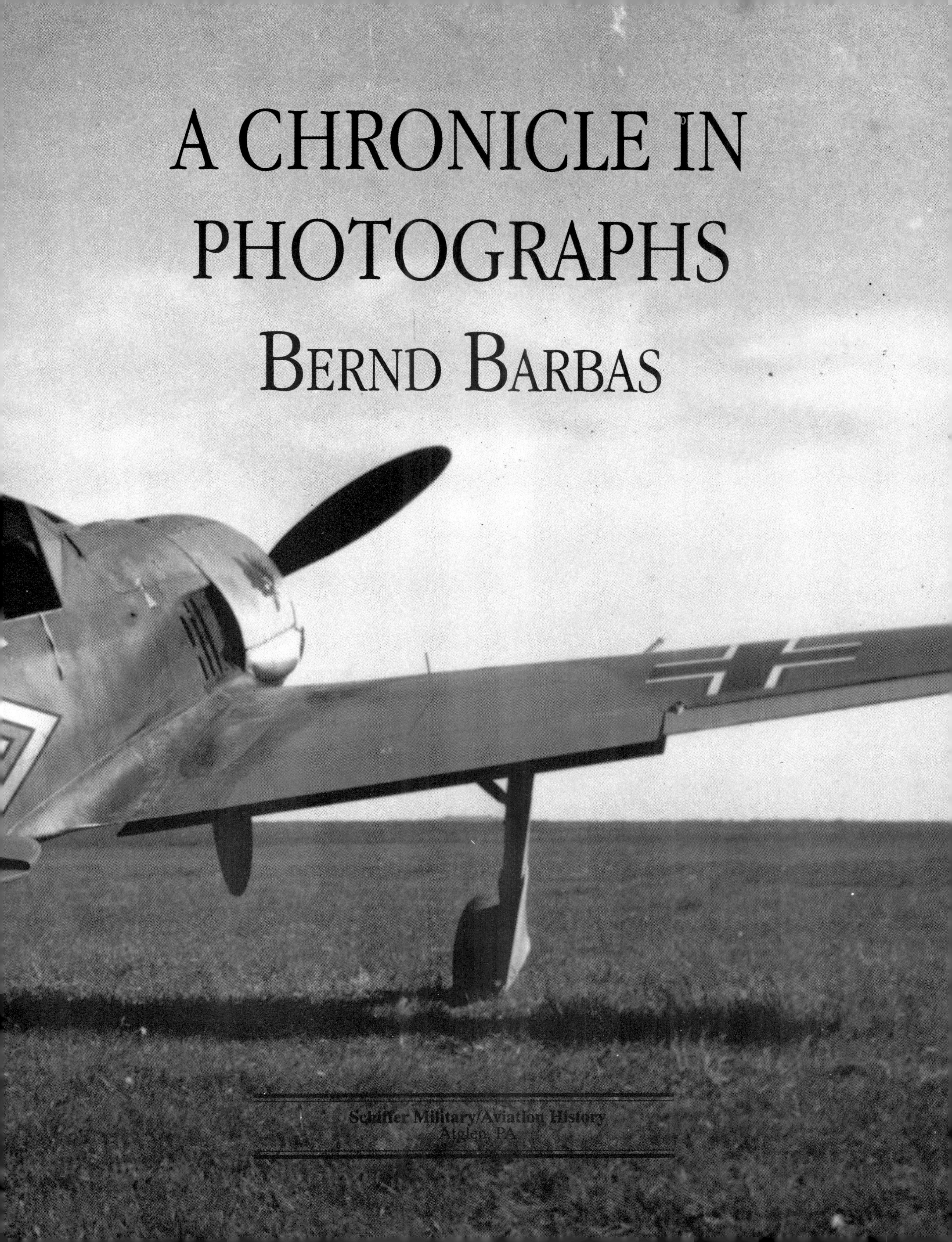

Schiffer Military/Aviation History
Atglen, PA

ACKNOWLEDGEMENTS

The author would like to express his thanks to all who have contributed to this undertaking; firstly to the late Erich Hartmann for writing the foreword, and to all those friends and associates who provided advice and information, especially: Jean-Yves Lorant, Peter Petrick, M. Rosenboom (of VFW-Fokker), J.B. Frappé, Jim Crow, Heinz Grass, Hans Lächler, F. Quinones, Richard P. Lutz, K.H. Faltermeier, Mr. Palecki, and many other, but especially to Paul Stipdonk who furnished so many pictures from his collection. Also to G. Aders, Ernst Obermaier, Hans Ring, Werner Girbig and Karl Ries, without whose work and cooperation this book would have been impossible to produce.

Thanks also go to all the *ex-Luftwaffe* personnel and their relatives who have made available their private photograph collections. These include: Mrs. Dörr and Mrs. Abelmann, Karl Demuth, Walter Giese, Hermann Graf, Kurt Bühligen, Lothar Busse, Erich Rudorffer, Wilhelm Vermeulen, Rudolph Schwaiger, Wolfgang Ewald, Ernst Laube, Martin Villing, Anton Hackl, Ernst Börngen, Hugo Dahmer, Franz Demattio, Werner Schroer, Gerhard Ille, Johannes Wiese, Walter Krupinski, Franz Reichenbach, Norbert Hannig, Heinz Schwertfeger, Karl Brill, Erwin Leykauf, Walter Loos, Hans Neuschütz, Dr. Otto Schürer, Hans Herrmann, Walter Horten, Ernst-Wilhelm Reinert, Zeno Bäumel, Karl Munz, Ernst Schröder, Fritz Treiber, Fritz Tegtmeier, and Herr Heizmann.

Additional information came from: Erich and Ursula Hartmann, Günther Rall, Gerhard Barkhorn, Peter Düttmann, Walter Schuck, Wilhelm Batz, Gustav Rödel, Dietrich Hrabak, Alfred Grislawski, Reinhard Seiler, the late Herbert Rollwage and Karl Schnörrer, Gerhard Thyben, Hans-Ekkehard Bob, Otto Kath, Kurt Dombacher, Ernst Düllberg, Erwin Fleig, Josef Haiböck, Dr. Heinz Lange, Helmut Mertens, Friedrich Karl Müller, Oskar Romm, Hermann Schleinhege, and Gerhard Stamp. Thanks are also due to Horst Amberg and the late Rolf Lehmann of the *Gemeinschaft der Jagdflieger* for their invaluable help and to Herr Schönemann of WAST, for information concerning the fate of several pilots. Further assistance come from Michael Payne, Dr. H.G. Mutke, Frank Smith, Thomas Hitchcock, Hermann Dorner, the US Army, and Hanfried Schliephake.

A particular mention should be made of the late *Gen.* Hannes Trautloft, a former *Kommodore* of JG 54, for his help in obtaining so many photographs of his old unit. The author would also like to pay particular credit to Richard Goyat who prepared the outstanding colored artwork and to Reinhard Sandow for his equally meticulous black and white drawings.

Finally, the author must pay tribute to the tolerance and help afforded not only by his publishers but also by his wife Christa who prepared the original typescript. In view of the limited information in some areas of research, the author will be most grateful to receive any further material and may be contacted at:

Primelweg 47
D 88662 Überlingen
Germany

Dust jacket artwork by Steve Ferguson, Colorado Springs, CO

STALINGRAD BLUE

Kommodore Major Wolf-Dietrich Wilcke of JG 3 *Udet* pulls his Bf 109G-2/R6 away from another victim during the battle of 1942 for Stalingrad. The summer offensive, known as Operation "Blue," was the high point in the annals of the *Jagdfliegern* as many an *Experten* reached the century mark of aerial victories over the Volga River valley.

On September 6, Wilcke scored his 100th kill, and as of December 17, he would be the fourth German fighter pilot to reach 150 victories, which produced the Oak Leaves and Swords over his Knight's Cross. However, the war on the battlefield below did not go well and by winter's end, Germany's entire 6th Army was lost at Stalingrad.

As the Wehrmacht fell into retreat throughout 1943, the various gruppen of JG 3 would simultaneously fight in Russia, Italy and in the Reich home defense. Despite the rigors of a command in disarray, *Oberst* Wilcke continued to lead missions against the Allied daylight bombardments and gained another twelve victories. On March 23, 1943, the odds of four years of continuous combat played out when the famous *kommodore* was shot down near Schoppenstedt, Germany, very likely by 4th Fighter Group P-51 aces Don Gentile and John Godfrey. Germany had lost a truly irreplaceable combat leader.

Book Design by MJ Hannigan

Library of Congress Catalog Number: 95-68642

Printed in China
ISBN: 0-88740-751-X

We are interested in hearing from authors with book ideas on related topics.

This title was originally published as *Planes of the Luftwaffe Fighter Aces Vol I,* by Kookaburra Technical Publications Pty. Ltd.

Published by Schiffer Publishing Ltd.
77 Lower Valley Road
Atglen, PA 19310
Please write for a free catalog.
This book may be purchased from the publisher.
Please include $2.95 postage.
Try your bookstore first.

CONTENTS

***Oblt* Erich Hartmann, the world's most successful fighter pilot with a tally of 352 victories. He is seen here with his mechanic Mertens and his Bf 109G-6.**

FOREWORD

When Bernd Barbas invited me to contribute the foreword to Aircraft of the Luftwaffe Fighter Aces, I was pleased and honored to accept the opportunity to do so.

Once I examined the early proofs I was surprised to see the extent and variety of the material he had managed to collect during his research. It quickly took me back to my earlier days as a wartime fighter pilot.

Looking back through photographs taken in those difficult times made me realize how young and innocent we were; yet despite this, many of us somehow managed to come through it all.

These days, however, it merely brings home to me the fact that so many of my contemporary airmen on both sides were not nearly so fortunate.

I also think of the great work our ground personnel performed, often under very difficult and exhausting conditions. This was especially true when airfields were a sea of mud or when it was necessary to work in the open during the unbelievably cold wintry weather on the Russian Front. What a fine example they set and what little acknowledgement they received!

When I look back and reflect upon the war years, I can only hope that today's youth will be spared the day-by-day experiences we lived through in those times.

I would like to record my gratitude to the author for the fine task he has performed, and commend his work as a valuable enrichment to the record of aerial warfare. It is also my wish that it may contribute something to mutual goodwill and international understanding amongst all who fly themselves of who are interested in aviation.

(Erich Hartmann)
1922-1993

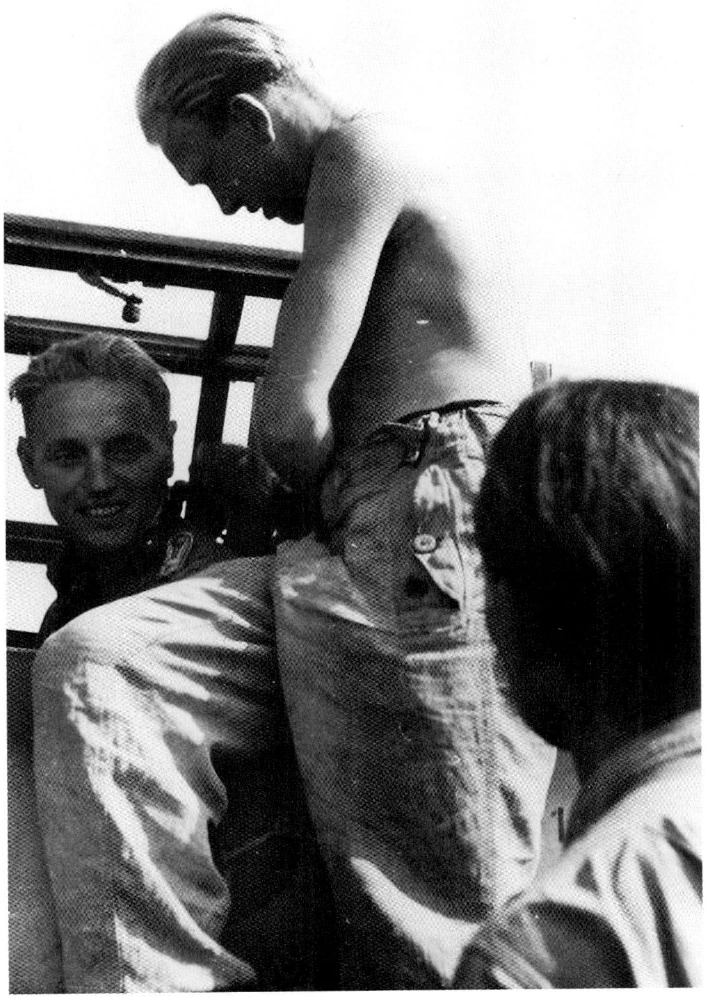

Hartmann in his Bf 109G-6 , "Yellow 1." With this aircraft he made his 300th victory on August 25, 1944. Also seen is his mechanic Mertens.

Aircraft of the Luftwaffe Fighter Aces I

Walter Oesau, *Kommodore* for JG 1 and for whom it was named after his death on May 11, 1944.

Chapter 1

JAGDGESCHWADER 1 "*OESAU*"

At the beginning of WW II only the staff of this unit existed, based at Jever in North-Western Germany and controlling aircraft drawn from other units. Its task was to defend the "German Bight" from attacks by the RAF . The unit operated during the invasions of Denmark and Norway in April 1940, and later in Netherlands and Northern France. At the end of 1940 the I./JG 1 based in the Netherlands. Returning from Russia in September 1941 as I./JG 3, the *Gruppe* was redesignated II./JG 1 and was one of the first units to receive the FW 190. By the end of 1941 there was a third *Gruppe,* based in Denmark and during Spring 1942, a fourth *Gruppe* was established. Both saw action over Northern Germany.

In April 1943 I. and III. *Gruppen* became JG 11. The fourth *Gruppe* became I./JG 1 and III. was re-formed in the Netherlands. During 1943, JG 1 constituted the backbone of Home Defense, countering the American daylight raids. After *the Kommodore,* Walter Oesau was killed, in combat with American P-38 Lightnings on May 11, 1944, the unit took his name, Oesau, as a title honor.

After D-Day in June 1944 the unit moved to France and by August had been virtually wiped out. Reestablished in November 1944, the unit resumed its home defense duties, based at Twenthe, Lengerich, and Rheine. On January 1, 1945, I./JG 1 attacked Maldeghem and II. *Gruppe*, St Denis Westrem while III. *Gruppe* supported I. *Gruppe.* Some aircraft of I./JG 1 also attacked Ursel. At a cost of 24 pilots lost, JG 1 claimed to have destroyed 32 Spitfires. Later in the month JG 1 was moved to Königsberg in the East, where it flew as air cover for Ju 52s supplying the Kurland pocket. When the Soviets overran the area, the unit was withdrawn. At Garz, on the island of Usedom, the Fw 190s of I. *Gruppe* were handed over to the pilots of II. *Gruppe* so that the former could train for conversion to the He 162 at Parchim and Ludwigslust during March. In April 1945 they went to Leck in Schleswig-Holstein where they were joined in May by II. *Gruppe*. The third *Gruppe* was disbanded.

Contrary to what has been previously reported in some publications, the He 162 did see combat and victory claims were made. Tactics were the same as for the Me 262, but owing to lack of fuel supplies, limitations on flight time, lack of fighter direction and the generally chaotic conditions, few operational sorties were flown. On May 4, 1945, I. and II. *Gruppen* were combined to become I.*(Einsatz)*/JG 1 under the command of *Maj.* Zober. Two days later British troops occupied the airfield.

A Fw 190 A-5, WNr. 1230, "Green 13" flown by Walter Oesau, shown here at Beaumont le Roger, France, around 1943. The rudder shows five aircraft silhouettes – this marking is either showing his 100+ victories, or five out of his fourteen downed bombers. (Happel)

Walter Oesau, *Kommodore,* JG 1, with his "Green 13." He reached his 100th victory on October 26, 1941.

Above: Three *Staffelkapitäne* of I./JG 1. From left to right: *Hpt* Wolfgang Ludewig, *Hpt* Heinz Künnecke and *Oblt* Karl Demuth. When this photograph was taken at Leck, Schleswig-Holstein, towards the end of the war, there were about 45 He 162s of I. *(Einsatz)* JG 1 in the background.

Below: In front of a partially painted He 162 are, from left, *Maj* Zober, *Obst* Ihlefeld, *Hpt* Künnecke, *Oblt* Demuth, *Hpt* Gallowitsch, *Hpt* Strassen, and *Hpt* Ludewig.

Left: Standing from left to right are *Hpt* Ludewig, *Hpt* Gallowitsch, *Oblt* Demuth, *Hpt* Künnecke and *Lt* Rudolph Schmitt, who was a *Staffelkapitän* of 1./JG 1.

***Lt* Karl Demuth, *Staffelkapitän* of 3./JG 1. His highest award was the *Deutsches Kreuz in Gold*.**

***Left: Oberstleutnant* Herbert Ihlefeld, *Kommodore* of JG 1, wearing the *Ritterkreuz mit Eichenlaub und Schwertern*.**

Above: Karl Demuth stands on the wing of his Fw 190, probably "Black 11," after a landing accident.

Right: Demuth surrounded by members of JG 1, in front of his Fw 190A-7, "Black 11," W Nr 642558. On March 6, 1944 he had to bail out over Minden after claiming two victories.

***Hpt* Hans Ehlers, *Gruppenkommandeur* of I./JG 1.**

Above: Ehlers' Fw 190A-4, W Nr 581 (?), carried the JG 1 emblem under the cockpit and the I. Gruppe emblem. Also seen in close-up (below), is the painted cowling.

"White 4" of I./JG 1 after a particularly heavy landing. The aircraft had several noticeable variations in its markings and camouflage.

Mechanics at a hangar door. In the background is a Fw 190 with black and white striped hood.

Their black and white striped cowlings still obvious despite the poor weather conditions, these Fw 190s of I./JG 1 prepare to take off.

A Fw 190A-6 of I./JG 1 under inspection during February 1944. On its back and white striped cowling was a variation of the JG 1 emblem.

"White 1" was Lt Rudolf Schmitt's He 162 at Leck. The differences in camouflage are interesting.

Hpt Heinz Künnecke with his He 162A-2, "Yellow 5." The diving eagle badge with its red and white background was probably the *Staffel* emblem of 2./JG 1. It was introduced by *Stkap* Gerhard Hanf, who transferred in from III/JG 77.

Line up of He 162s of the JG1 in Leck, waiting for British troops in May 1945.

"White 1" in front, followed by "Yellow 5" with the cockpit cover of "White 11." The only men identified here are Künnecke standing at the far left, Demuth 3rd from the left and Ludewig who stands 2nd from the right.

One of the many He 162s surrendered at Leck in May 1945. On the far left seems to be *Maj* Zober with Demuth standing to his right.

Heinz "Heino" Hanke standing beside his Fw 190A-3, W Nr 0495.

Heino Hanke after he bailed out over Denmark.

Heino Hanke wearing the jacket of a "Miss Behavin" crew member. Jacket showsg eighteen mission markings. Hanke had changed the jacket with Mr. Markussen the B-17 co-pilot, on February 20, 1944 in Odense, Denmark.

Above: Hanke's distinctive Fw 190A-3, W Nr 0495, photographed when he was *Gruppenadjudant* of I./JG 1. The color scheme is believed to have been a 71/02 combination. The unit emblem can be seen under the windscreen. Below: Close up of the above aircraft.

Heino Hanke in Bf 109 E "White 6." On the cowling are two of the always needed "black men."

Heino Hanke and two of his ground crew with his Bf 109 E, "White 6," at Leuwaarden in 1940. The camouflage on the upper surfaces was probably mainly dark green 71.

Above and below: Another aircraft flown by Hanke was the Bf 109F "Black 7," whose number's thin white outline had only been half finished. The aircraft had standard grey comouflage.

***Oberstleutnant* Egon Mayer with *"Eichenlaub zum Ritterkreuz"* as *Kommodore* of JG 2.**

Chapter 2

JAGDGESCHWADER 2 *"RICHTHOFEN"*

At the outbreak of war only the *Geschwaderstab* and I. *Gruppe* of JG 2 existed. Only 1 *Staffel* saw action during the Polish campaign, and in November 1939 the unit moved to Frankfurt/Main. With the second and third *Gruppen* formed during 1940, the *Geschwader* served in the West until 1943. Together with JG 26, the unit was heavily engaged in the Dieppe landing in August 1942, JG 2 reequipped with the Fw 190A-2 with the exception of 2.*Staffel* which flew the Bf 109G-1 from Ligescourt under the control of JG 26. The *Stab* and I./JG 2 were at Triqueville with 35 aircraft, II./JG 2 was at Beaumont-le-Roger with 25 aircraft and III./JG 2 at Cherbourg-Maupertus with 40 aircraft. Over Dieppe on the 19th of August, the pilots of JG 2 and JG 26 claimed 106 victories, of which 98 were fighters. JG 2 lost 12 aircraft, plus 10 damaged; meanwhile JG 26 lost seven, plus one damaged.

During November 1942 the second *Gruppe* moved to Sicily and in March 1943 to Tunisia. 11. *Staffel* also moved to Sicily and was absorbed by JG 53. The remainder of JG 2 was meanwhile hard pressed in France. I. *Gruppe* moved to Italy in February 1944 to operate over the Anzio/Nettuno beachheads. After D-Day on June 6, 1944, the unit was almost annihilated by overwhelming Allied air superiority. In August the *Geschwader* was reestablished in Germany, but there was no respite. On January 1, 1945, with the Fw 190F-8s of SG 4, the aircraft of JG 2 attacked St Trond in Belgium, a former *Luftwaffe* night-fighter base which was at this time occupied by the P-47 Thunderbolts of the American 48th and 404th Fighter Groups.

I. and III. *Gruppen* had been reequipped with brand-new Fw 190D-9s and II. *Gruppe* with AS-engined Bf 109s, G-14 and K-4 models. Many Allied aircraft were destroyed on their airfields, but at a cost of 23 pilots killed or missing, ten taken prisoner and four wounded. During April, JG 2 moved from Frankfurt to Munich and it was here that the unit ended the war.

Framed by the undercarriage legs of another Bf 109F were two other aircraft, "White 1" and "White 7," both flown by Egon Mayer, Staffelkapitän of 7./JG 2. The victory markings of the former machine are barely visible.

Egon Mayer in front of his Bf 109F.

Bf 109F "White 1" of Egon Mayer, Staffelkapitän of 7/JG 2. Photographs of this aircraft were previously published, but without victory markings. "White 7" was also used by Egon Mayer.

Above photos taken in Engen/Hegau. Top: Egon Mayer on the right visiting his mother with Hermann Graf on the left who was also there on leave. Below: Mayer and Graf in Engen, probably in the restaurant "Zur Linde."

Bf 109F, W Nr 6720, Egon Mayer's "White 1." The rudder had been painted yellow and indicated one French and twenty-two British aircraft shot down.

Hauptmann Hans Hahn with *"Eichenlaub."*

"Assi" Hahn, *Gruppenkommandeur* of II./JG 54, climbing out of his Bf 109F on November 19, 1941.

Two shots of the rudders of *Oblt* Hans (Assi) Hahn, *Staffelkapitän* of 4./JG 2. The photograph on the left shows twenty victories. The photograph on the right was taken on November 19, 1941, after he had been awarded the *Eichenlaub* for 42 victories when with III./JG 2 in the West.

Above and below: *Hauptmann* Hans "Assi" Hahn, *Gruppenkommandeur* of III./JG 2, and his Fw 190A-3, W Nr 223, in Beaumont le Roger, France.

"Assi" Hahn and his bear "Wumm." During late evenings at the JG 54 camp, the bear was given a pair of gloves and "boxed" with pilots. Hahn was the only pilot who could defeat the bear.

Above and below: On May 4, 1942, "Assi" Hahn reached his 60th victory. The rudder shows 61 of his 108 victories (68 in the West).

Oberleutnant Siegfried Schnell with *"Eichenlaub zum Ritterkreuz."*

Oberleutnant Schnell and comrade looking at his aircraft.

Below: The spotlessly clean and very new Fw 190A-4, W Nr 764, "Yellow 4," of Siegfried Schnell of 9./JG 2. It had grey comouflage and a colorfully adorned yellow rudder.

Ofw Siegfried Schnell pictured in 1940 looking at the tail of his Bf 109E, W Nr 1232. The rudder, which had been repainted yellow, displays sixteen victories.

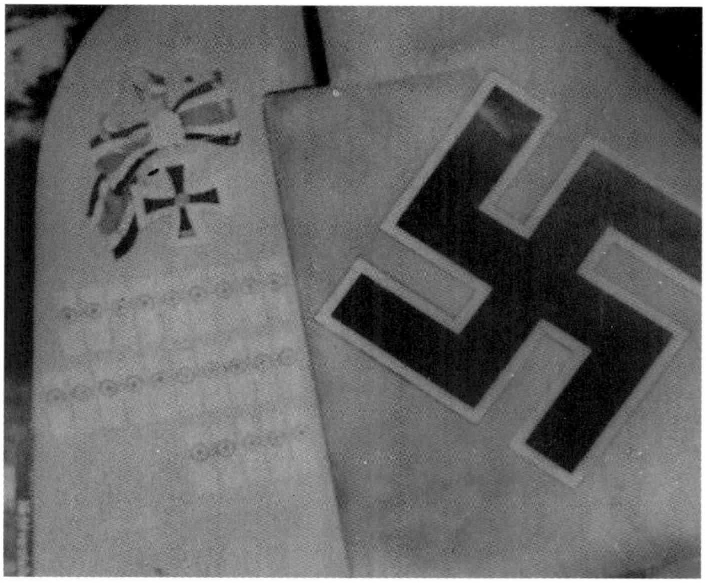

Sixty-four victories are displayed on the rudder of Siegfried Schnell's Fw 190A-3. As Staffelkapitän of 9./JG 2, he received the *Eichenlaub* on July 9, 1941 for his first forty victories (the bars all show RAF roundels).

Above: Siegfried Schnell with several of his pilots in June 1942 at Théville on the Cherbourg Peninsula.

Left: Oberleutnant Schnell seems to be satisfied.

Ofw **Werner Machold painting the ninth victory bar on his aircraft (his previous tally included six French machines and three British). The interesting brush-applied speckled camouflage was typical of the unit.**

Machold again, this time with twenty-one victories displayed on what appears to have been a rather crudely repainted yellow rudder.

Above and above right: This Bf 109F, "White 8," was the machine of Kurt Goltzsch of 7./JG 2. The name under the cockpit seems to be Anni.

Above: *Maj* Kurt Bühligen claimed his 100th victory, a P-47 Thunderbolt, on June 9, 1944. Here he is being congratulated at Creil, France by *Obstlt* Josef Priller of JG 26.

Right: Josef Wurmheller's Fw 190A, W Nr 7334, showing the *Ritterkreuz mit Eichenlaub* for his first sixty victories, plus a further fifteen, including five four-engine bombers. The photograph was taken at Vannes in July 1943. From the left: *Fw* Kopp, *Oblt* Wurmheller, and *Fw* Bleyer.

These four photographs are of Bf 109E-4, W Nr 5344, belonging to the famous *Major* Helmut Wick, *Kommodore* of JG 2, *"Richthofen."* The rudder shows fifty-four victories. The aircraft was heavily re-camouflaged with a dabbed-sponge technique and also re-marked from *"dual chevron"* to *Kommodore*. With a total of fifty-six victories in the West (the leading ace of the *Luftwaffe,* passing both Galland and Mölders). Wick was fatally shot down south of the Isle of Wight on November 28, 1940.

The aircraft shown here was Erich Rudorffer's Bf 109F, "Yellow 9," of 6./JG 2, photographed at Abbeville-Drucat during the summer of 1941. When engine cowlings required recamouflaging, this was often done when detached from the rest of the airframe for greater convenience.

The tail of "Yellow 9," Taken at Beaumont-le-Roger in early 1942, it is known to have had the then unusual 71/02/65 camouflage scheme; a yellow rudder, a black or black-green spinner, and an unusually long second *Gruppe* bar.

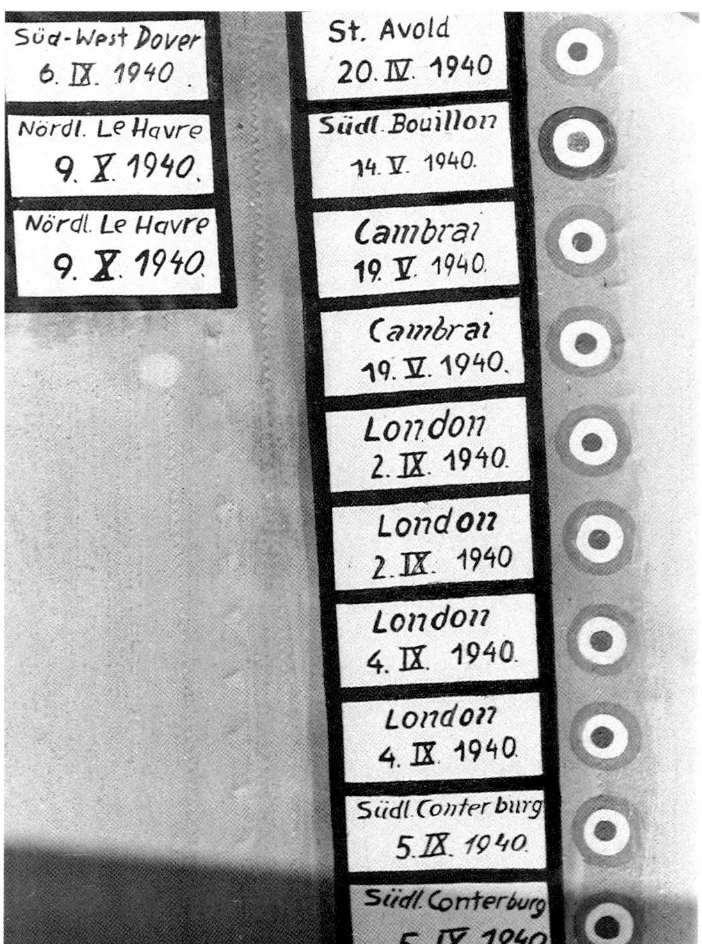

"Yellow 9," *Motti*, a similarly camouflaged Bf 109E of 3./JG2, in early 1940. On the far right was Rudi Pflanz, who was to claim fifty-two victories.

Left: Rudder of Bf 109E of *Kommandeur* III/JG 2 Otto Bertram showing thirteen victories. For these he received the *Ritterkreuz* on October 28, 1940.

The yellow rudder of this grey-camouflaged Bf 109F of JG 2, "White 12," shows two victories.

An unidentified Bf 109F of II./*Gruppe*. Its yellow rudder displays eight victories.

This photograph shows the *Hahn* (Cockerel) emblem of III./*Gruppe* on the cowling of Fw 190, "White 9," of 7./JG 2.

Facinating photograph of several Bf 109Es of III./JG 2 taken as their engines were being serviced. The nearest aircraft being is that of the *Gruppenadjutant*. The badge on the cowling in the foreground is that of 7. *Staffel.*

A Bf 109F, W Nr 7558, in the "Kommodore" markings belonging to Oesau.

A Bf 109F, W Nr 7554, taken at St Pol, France in 1941. also with the "Kommodore" markings belonging to Oesau.

Above: In this photograph, taken in November 1941, the oxygen bottles of this Bf 109F of JG 2 are being replenished.

Left: A seat parachute pack ready for immediate operational use.

Mechanics or "black men" as they were called, working on another Bf 109F. The apertures for the engine guns are plainly shown.

Bf 109G-10, W Nr 150816 of 5./JG 2, at Langensalza, Germany, in April 1945.

Above and below: Taken in North Africa in the spring of 1942, these two photographs show Franz Schwaiger and his Bf 109F, "Yellow 3" of 6./JG 3. With Schwaiger is his friend Sepp Weber. Details of interest are the II. *Gruppe* emblem, the armored windscreen, the less faded tan 79 camouflage on the wing and the red "Don't walk" lettering. *Gisela* was the name of Schwaiger's girlfriend.

Chapter 3

Jagdgeschwader 3 "*Udet*"

In September 1939 this unit consisted of only a *Stab* and I. *Gruppe*, II. and III. *Gruppen* not being added until the spring of 1940. After playing an important part in the French campaign and the Battle of Britain in the latter months of 1940, the unit was transferred to the East in June 1941 to take part in Operation *Barbarossa.* Following the advance into Russia, JG 3 moved forward from airfield to airfield. By October 1941, II. *Gruppe* was operating over the Crimea and at about the same time the first *Gruppe* was reconstituted. At the end of the year the entire *Geschwader* was withdrawn to Wiesbaden to rest and refit and it was at this time that the name Udet was adopted. Early in 1942, II. *Gruppe* moved to Sicily and North Africa for operations over Malta, while III. *Gruppe* went to the northern sector of the Russian Front.

The whole unit became involved in the battle for Stalingrad and one well-known pilot of JG 3, Georg Schentke (90 victories), a member of the *Platzschutzstaffel Pitomnik,* had to abandon his aircraft on Christmas Day. Landing behind the Russian lines, he was reported as missing in action. During 1943 the fighting was concentrated between the rivers Don and Donetz, over the Kuban and around Kursk where the great tank battle raged. I. *Gruppe* went home to Germany in the spring, followed in August by the remainder of the *Geschwader.* The Stab and I. *Gruppe* operated Bf 109s over western Germany, II. *Gruppe* over the Netherlands and III. *Gruppe* over southern Germany. A newly-formed IV. *Gruppe* remained for a while in Italy, but returned to the homeland to fly the heavily armored *Sturmböcke* – the Fw 190A-8. In June 1944, the *Stab,* II. and III. *Gruppen* were thrown against the invasion forces in Normandy and suffered heavily. Withdrawn to Germany, they again operated over the Ardennes battlefield in December 1944.

On January 1, 1945, the whole unit took off at first light from airfields in the Paderborn area. Their targets were the airfields of Eindhoven and Gilze Rijen where more than 11 Allied fighter squadrons were based. Heinz Bär, in his Fw 190A-9, claimed two Typhoons to bring his score to 204. Many Allied aircraft were destroyed, but at a cost of ten German pilots killed and six captured. Once more JG 3 returned to the East for the last battle for Berlin; but the war had been lost and the unit was disbanded in Northern Germany. Werner Schroer, the last *Kommodore*, has stated to the author that the complete records of JG 3 lie buried somewhere near the old airfield at Pasewalk.

Franz Schwaiger sitting in front of his "Yellow 3." II. *Gruppe* bar is also painted yellow.

Schwaiger, in earlier days, with his flying teacher in front of a Klemm training aircraft.

Franz Schwaiger and his mechanics with "Yellow 3."

As a new pilot in Pilzen, a very young Franz Schwaiger.

Schwaiger in tropical uniform in front of his tent.

Above: Another shot of Schwaiger, second from right, with II./JG 3 in Russia. Second from the left is Otto Wessling, another holder of the Knight's Cross.

Left: Franz Schwaiger wearing the *Ritterkreuz*. The Bf 109G-6/R6 pictured here, covered by black oil, bears the adopted emblem of JG 3, a stylized red winged letter U (for Udet) on a white shield.

Oberfeldwebel Franz Schwaiger left, talking with another *Ritterkreuzträger* of JG 3, *Leutnant* Otto Wessling, who received the *Ritterkreuz* for fifty victories nearly two months earlier as did Schwaiger, in Russia.

Franz Schwaiger as the only *Ritterkreuzträger* surrounded by *Luftwaffe* comrades in front of "Haus Florida" in Bad Wiessee/ Tegernsee during holidays in December 1942. Left of Schwaiger is Adolf Glunz, famous JG 26 pilot. Fifth from the right is Wolf Ettel another famous pilot of JG 3, 124 victories and winner of the *Eichenlaub*.

Feldwebel Franz Schwaiger with *Ritterkreuz, Frontflugspange, EK and Flugzeugführerabzeichen.*

The grave of *Ritterkreuzträger Leutnant* Franz Schwaiger, in Ochsenhausen

Above and right: This winter camouflaged Bf 109G-2 is believed to have been flown by Kurt Brändle, *Gruppenkommandeur* of II./JG 3. To the right is a nose view of the same aircraft.

This Bf 109F in startling three color camouflage was "Yellow 4," flown by *Ofw* Eberhard von Boremski. It had forty-three victory bars, for which he received the *Ritterkreuz* on May 3, 1942, and carried the name *Maxi* near the cockpit.

Above: Hauptmann Gordon Gollob with *Eichenlaub zum Ritterkreuz* as *Gruppenkommandeur* of II./JG 3 in 1941.

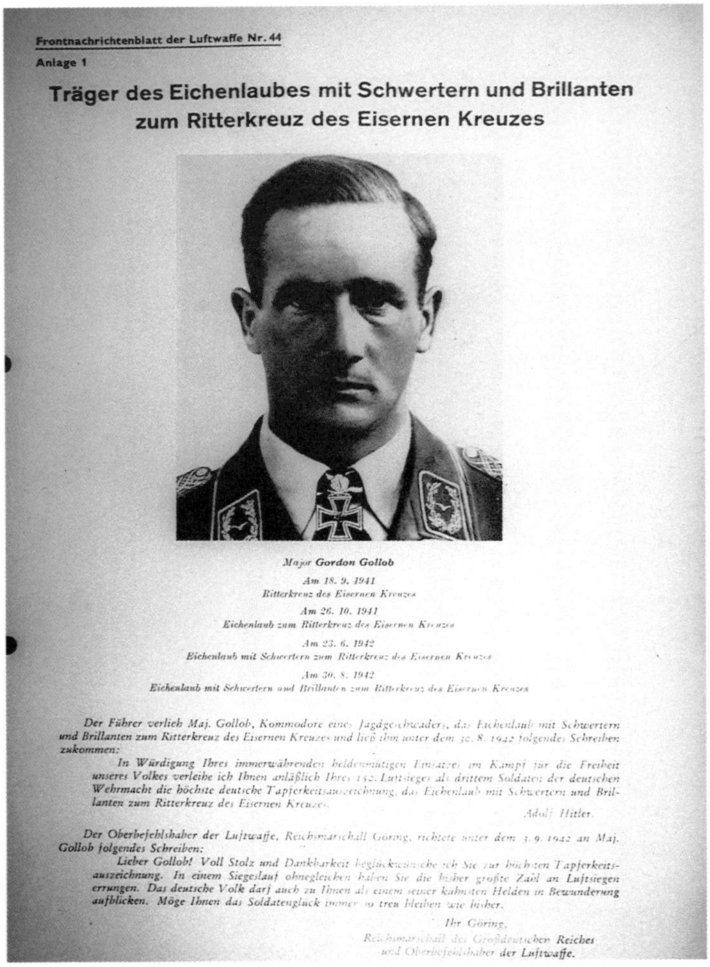

Frontnachrichtenblatt der Luftwaffe Nr. 44

Anlage 1

Träger des Eichenlaubes mit Schwertern und Brillanten zum Ritterkreuz des Eisernen Kreuzes

Major **Gordon Gollob**

Am 18. 9. 1941
Ritterkreuz des Eisernen Kreuzes

Am 26. 10. 1941
Eichenlaub zum Ritterkreuz des Eisernen Kreuzes

Am 23. 6. 1942
Eichenlaub mit Schwertern zum Ritterkreuz des Eisernen Kreuzes

Am 30. 8. 1942
Eichenlaub mit Schwertern und Brillanten zum Ritterkreuz des Eisernen Kreuzes

Der Führer verlieh Maj. Gollob, Kommodore eines Jagdgeschwaders, das Eichenlaub mit Schwertern und Brillanten zum Ritterkreuz des Eisernen Kreuzes und ließ ihm unter dem 30. 8. 1942 folgendes Schreiben zukommen:

In Würdigung Ihres immerwährenden heldenmütigen Einsatzes im Kampf für die Freiheit unseres Volkes verleihe ich Ihnen anläßlich Ihres 150. Luftsieges als drittem Soldaten der deutschen Wehrmacht die höchste deutsche Tapferkeitsauszeichnung, das Eichenlaub mit Schwertern und Brillanten zum Ritterkreuz des Eisernen Kreuzes.

Adolf Hitler.

Der Oberbefehlshaber der Luftwaffe, Reichsmarschall Göring, richtete unter dem 3. 9. 1942 an Maj. Gollob folgendes Schreiben:

Lieber Gollob! Voll Stolz und Dankbarkeit beglückwünsche ich Sie zur höchsten Tapferkeitsauszeichnung. In einem Siegeslauf ohnegleichen haben Sie die bisher größte Zahl an Luftsiegen errungen. Das deutsche Volk darf auch zu Ihnen als einem seiner kühnsten Helden in Bewunderung aufblicken. Möge Ihnen das Soldatenglück immer so treu bleiben wie bisher.

Ihr Göring,
Reichsmarschall des Großdeutschen Reiches und Oberbefehlshaber der Luftwaffe.

Top right: *"Frontnachrichtenblatt"* showing *Major* Gordon Gollob after he was awarded with the *"Brillianten."* He received this decoration for reaching his 150th victory, on August 29, 1942 – a number no one believed could be reached.

Right: *Hpt* Gordon Gollob preparing for a sortie in his Bf 109E during 1940.

These two photographs were taken on October 7, 1940 and show *Maj* Günther Lützow, JG 3 *Kommodore* on the left and *Hpt* Wilhelm Balthasar, *Gruppenkommandeur*, next to the tail of Lützows Bf109E which shows his thirty-eight victories.

Hauptmann Lützow, as *Kommodore*, coming home from aerial combat on August 30, 1940. With thirteen victories already on the rudder he accomplished two more in this Bf 109F-4.

Right and center right: These two photographs show *Hpt* Wilhelm Balthasar, *Gruppenkommandeur* of III./JG 3 climbing out of his aircraft after returning from a mission on November 4, 1940, when he claimed four victories. This was accomplished even though he left the hospital a few days earlier, still recovering from some serious wounds.

Above: Two Bf 109G-2/R6 fighters flown by Wolf-Dietrich Wilcke, both with identical markings. By this time, late 1942, their 74/75/76 scheme was standard camouflage. Both carried the JG 3 badge on their cowlings.

Right: Another shot of both aircraft. Note used propeller blades and partially removed wheel strut covers. Also of interest are the aluminum colored spokes of the main wheels.

Below and below right: *Maj* Wolfgang Ewald with *Obst* Wolf-Dietrich Wilcke, on the right. Wilcke wears the *Eichenlaub mit Schwertern,* awarded for his 155 victories up to December 1942.

Maj Wolfgang Ewald photographed in Russia during the spring of 1943, when he was *Gruppenkommandeur* of III./JG 3. His final tally was seventy-eight victories. In July he was shot down by Russian flak and spent many years as a POW.

Above and below: Both photographs show *Major* Ewald in the cockpit of a Bf 109G.

Maj Ewald in the center and Lützow on the left, in front of a Bf 109F. The aircraft had additional front window armor.

Ewald testing a new grey camouflaged Bf 109G-4 in early 1943 in Russia. Its markings implied a combination of the functions of *Gruppenkommandeur* and *Kommodore*, who at the time was Wilcke. The aircraft had spoked wheels with narrow tires and wheel bumps on the wings. Traces of its overpainted radio call sign, M+M, are just visible.

***Major* Ewald and his mechanics after landing his Bf 109G-1. Chevrons are slightly visible in both photographs .**

***Oberleutnant* Lützow, center, *Major* Ewald, left, and others in a discussion on a Russian airfield during the summer of 1942.**

Feldwebel Strebel with his Bf 109K-4 , "White 4," of 9./JG 3 in March 1945. The simplified antenna mounting and C3 fuel sign are clearly shown. Like many K models, it was probably painted in a combination of late-war greens.

Aircraft and members of 6./JG 3 in front of "Arco dei Fileni."

Two Fw 190D-9s of the Staff of IV./JG 3. Their numbers, 1 and 2 respectively, were probably in the dark blue staff colors.

Uffz Maximowitz of IV./JG 3, in his Fw 190A-8/R2, "Black 8."

Above and below: Bearing the single chevron markings of an adjutant, this Fw 190D-9 was flown on occasions by Oskar Romm, *Gruppenkommandeur* of IV./JG 3.

Another machine flown by Oskar Romm, this one had two black chevrons thinly outlined in white. It probably bore an 81/82/76 camouflage scheme.

A very rare, all light grey camouflaged, Bf 109G-6 AS, W Nr 412179, Black 14 belonging to *Fw* Horst Petschler of 2./JG 3. On May 30, 1944 his friend Otto Büssow was killed in this machine while engaged in a dogfight near Bielitz.

Pilots of the 14./JG 4 standing in front of their command post. From left: *Unteroffizier* Beck, *Unteroffizier* Dittrich, *Oberfeldwebel* Babucke, *Unteroffizier* Blumenberg, *Unteroffizier* Müller, *Obergefreiter* Kestner and *Obergefreiter* Grüning.

Chapter 4

JAGDGESCHWADER 4

This fighter unit was formed in Romania at the beginning of 1943, with the establishment of only the first *Gruppe*. Its first major action took place on August 1, 1943 when a force of American B-24 Liberators attacked the Ploesti oil installations. From late 1943 until August 1944, JG 4 served in Italy. During the spring of 1944, a unit *Stab* was established at Kassel and this eventually became the *Geschwaderstab,* since a second *Gruppe* was formed under *Major* von Kornatzki at this time and elements of a third *Gruppe* had already existed since October 1943. II. *Gruppe* was equipped with the heavily armored Fw 190s known as *Sturmböcke*. Most of the illustrations relating to JG 4 show the aircraft of IV. *Gruppe* which had previously been II./JG 5.

Owing to the overwhelming Allied air superiority over France during the invasion period, no concerted action by the whole of JG 4 was possible, and in the autumn of 1944 the *Geschwader* withdrew eastward to take up home defence duties. It also took part in the Ardennes battle at the end of the year. On January 1, 1945, 55 aircraft of JG 4 took off from the Frankfurt area, a mixture of Fw 190A-8s and Bf 109G-10s, G-14s and K-4s, to attack the airfield at Le Coulot, south of Brussels. For JG 4, Operation *Bodenplatte* was a disaster. The target could not be found and instead the aircraft were widely dispersed and joined in the attacks on other targets with machines from other units. Twenty-three pilots were lost and II. *Gruppe* was virtually wiped out. *Gefreiter* Walter Wagner of 5. *Staffel,* for example, landed his Fw 190, badly damaged by groundfire, at St Trond airfield. In mid-January the unit moved to the Eastern Front to operate over the river Oder where the Russians were crossing, but in April it was sent north where the *Geschwader* was disbanded at Leck, Schleswig-Holstein.

These two photographs show *Gefreiter* Walter Wagner's Fw 190A-8, "White 11" of 5./JG 4. The aircraft is shown after an emergency landing on St Trond airfield on January 1, 1945. It carried a camouflage of 74/75/76. After being repainted it was later flown by American pilots of the 404th Fighter Group.

Unteroffizier **Walter Giese.**

***Uffz* Walter Giese of 14./JG 4 seated on his faithful "Black 8," a Bf 109G-14/AS, at Riesa-Leutewitz on October 1944.**

Above: Heavily camouflaged AS engined Bf 109 on a JG 4 airfield.

Below: This photograph was taken at Rheinsdorf near Jüterbog in October 1944 and shows Beck with one of his mechanics in front of a Bf 109G-14/AS. The black and white spiral spinners had been intoduced the previous July as identification markings.

These two photographs show *Unteroffizier* Beck and his Bf 109G-14. He was killed in action in his "Black 1" on December 3, 1944.

Beck again, this time with what looks like a "White 13," showing clearly the prominent bulged fairing on the upper cowling which covered the breech blocks and spent shells channel of the larger MG 131 armament.

Above: Ernst Scheufele at first flew cover for the Kriegsmarine, but later joined II./JG 5 and served in the East. He then transferred to IV./JG 4 flying home defense duties under *Kommodore* Michalski. On December 3, 1944 he was shot down by groundfire from an American supply unit near Aachen. He had a total of eighteen victories, including three four-engine bombers and two P-51 Mustangs.

Left: Uffz Beck and *Uffz* Dittrich (who was killed in action in his "Black 5" on December 5, 1944) in front of *Oblt* Scheufele's "Black 13" of 14./JG 4. Scheufele's girlfriend's nickname Peterle was painted yellow on the left side of the cockpit.

Kurt Esser standing in front of his Bf 109G-10. Of interest are the oil cooler, wider propellor blades, and the carefully applied spiral on the spinner.

This shot of *Hpt* Laube with his Bf 109G-10, "White 3", shows the wavy line of IV. Gruppe painted over the rear fuselage bands.

Above: *Reichsfähnrich* Kurt Esser leaning on the turbo-charger intake of his Bf 109G-10. Note the modified shape of the intake for this AS engined machine.

Right: Kurt Esser, with his mechanic, standing in front of his Bf 109G-10. The emblem of the old 6./JG 5 now served 14./JG 4.

On July 25, 1944, *Hauptmann* Theodor Weissenberger, *Gruppenkommandeur* of I/JG 5, had just made his 200th victory, on the invasion front, when he shot down a Spitfire southeast of Rouen. It was his 375th front fight. Coming from the eastern front as *Gruppenkommandeur* of II/JG 5, with 175 victories under his belt, he added twenty-five more victories in the west within six weeks, all of them against Allied Thunderbolts, Lightnings, Typhoons, Spitfires and Mustangs.

Everyone gathers to congratulate *Hauptmann* Weissenberger who had just climbed out of his aircraft at Frières airfield, France. During this flight he shot down two Spitfires within two minutes, his 199th and 200th victories. His mechanic "Mors" is seen atop the aircraft.

Chapter 5

JAGDGESCHWADER 5 "EISMEER"

First established in January 1942 in Norway as I./JG 5, this unit was to have an eventful history. The initial Gruppe comprised elements drawn from I./JG 77, 14./JG 77, and 2./ZG 76, and was to be responsible for the fighter cover of the entire Norwegian coast as far as Petsamo and for defense against Russian bombers from Murmansk. The extreme weather conditions within the Arctic Circle presented an exceptional challenge to men and machines. In May 1942, a Geschwaderstab was formed in Petsamo, and Jagdgruppe zbV (special duties) at Petsamo became II./JG 5. The third Gruppe came from IV./JG 1 which had formed at Brest in France in January. They came to Petsamo and Kirkenes in April 1942. Another Gruppe was formed in the summer to defend Southern Norway, later to be joined by 13. (Z).JG 5 and 14.(Jabo)/JG 5 flying Fw 190As. Operations were mainly concerned with countering the Allied convoys to Murmansk and interrupting the Russian railway link from the port to the Front.

II./JG 5 moved to the Russian Front in November 1943 and eventually became IV./JG 4. I./JG 5 moved during the same period to the Balkans, before joining in home defense operations. After a short spell in France after the invasion in June 1944, there was a return to home defense and redesignation as III./JG 6 in October 1944. 14./JG 5 went to Italy in April 1944 and became 4./SG 4, and 13./JG 5 was detached to become 10./ZG 26.

The Stab and III./JG 5 remained in Norway and were joined in August 1944 by IV. Gruppe which moved northward. On September 3, 1944, the Finnish Government initiated armistice negotiations with the Soviets and these were concluded on the 19th. Meanwhile, the Russian advance had reached Petsamo and in the operations here until October 9th, JG 5 claimed to have destroyed 85 enemy aircraft, including the unit's 3000th victim. By October 23rd, however, the last JG 5 pilot had left Kirkenes, and IV. Gruppe left for Stavanger without their machines, to be reequipped with Bf 109G-6s. IV. Gruppe moved to Bardufoss to obtain Fw 190s. The blackest day for JG 5 was November 12, 1944, when RAF Lancasters sank the German battleship Tirpitz in Sandnessund near Tromsö with "Tallboy" bombs. Nearly 1,000 German sailors died and Ehrler, Kommodore of JG 5, was court-martialled and convicted, although it had been impossible to intercept the bombers due to incorrect reporting and because they were flown over neutral Sweden.

JG 5 took no part in Operation Bodenplatte on January 1, 1945, but moved to Alesund in the south. But at the end of March a final combat with British naval aircraft brought four victory claims and three losses, the war ending for the unit in Andalsnes, Bergen and Stavanger.

Within minutes the aircraft, probably a Bf 109G-6, was camouflaged and stored away as the air was overcrowded with Allied aircraft. The aircraft has a spiral black and white spinner, 74/75/76 camouflage, dual chevron markings, and a 300 litre drop tank. The Balkenkreuz was of the old style with black borders.

Hpt Weissenberger, center, walking away from his Bf 109G on Frières airfield in France on July 25, 1944.

Comrades share in the victory by escorting Weissenberger across the airfield.

Hpt Weissenberger with his "*Eichenlaub zum Ritterkreuz.*"

Weissenberger with "200" sign and 200 victory map.

Weissenberger, with "200" sign, and comrades celebrating his victory. His friend Gerlach is holding the 200 victory map.

A close-up of the 200 victory map shows the English Channel with congratulations, *"Unserem Kommandeur Herrn Hauptmann Weissenberger – herzlichsten Glückwunsch zum 200 Luftsieg – I/Jagdgeschwader 5 Im Westen Juli 44."* (*Kommandeur Hpt* Weissenberger – hearty congratulations to your 200th air victory – I/ JG 5 in the west in July of 44).

Above and right: The staff building of the I/JG 5 in Frières, France. In the photo above note the map of beachheads hanging on the wall to the left. In the photo to the right the sign says *Gruppen-gefechtsstand.*

Hauptmann Schmidt and *Feldwebel* Schuck flying cover for an aircraft with *Generaloberst* Stumpff in the fall of 1943. At this time Schmidt was *Staffelkapitän* of 9./JG 5 and Schuck was his wingman. Schmidt flew "White 5" and Schuck "White 1", both Bf 109Gs.

Feldwebel Schuck climbing out of his Bf 109F, which probably had a yellow code.

Left and below: *Leutnant* Walter Schuck with his *"Eichenlaub zum Ritterkreuz."* He received this decoration on September 30, 1944 for 171 victories. With a total of 206 victories he was one of the top aces of JG 5.

From left: Schuck, Dörr, and Steinbach

Left Dörr and Schuck on the right sitting in the sun during the winter.

Bf 109E, "Yellow 8", of 7./JG 5 at Bodö, Norway during the winter of 1941-42. The aircraft, along with "Yellow 4", at that time was flown by Franz Dörr.

Oblt Franz Dörr, who was credited with 128 victories, perched on the cockpit ledge of his Bf 109G. It is clear that a previous marking had been under the forward of the fuselage since it was repainted, probably in grey 74.

Hauptmann Franz Dörr, Gruppenkommandeur of III./JG 5.

Dörr as *Hauptmann*.

The three photographs to the right show Dörr on the left and Philipp on the right, with "Yellow 4" and "Yellow 8" of 7./JG 5 in the foreground.

Oblt Dörr with *Ritterkreuz* which he had received on August 19, 1944 for ninety-five victories. While with JG 5 he scored 122 victories, and a total of 128.

Franz Dörr, on the left, talking to another pilot in front of a Bf 109G bearing an unusual "scribble" pattern.

Dörr on the left.

Above: Jakob "Jockel" Norz climbing out of his Bf 109G, "Black 8." At first, Norz flew with III./JG 5, 6./JG 5 and later with II./JG 5.

Right: Jakob Norz being decorated by *Luftflottenchef, Generaloberst* Stumpff.

Below: Jakob Norz in front of his faithful "Black 8", a Bf109G. Norz flew with II./JG 5 and was decorated with the *Ritterkreuz* by the *Luftflottenchef, Genobst* Stumpff. His final victory tally was 117.

Maj Heinrich Ehrler with *Eichenlaub*. With a minimum of 204 victories he was also one of the top aces of JG 5.

Ehrler in his car.

Above: A very interesting rudder photo, showing a total of 115 victories. At this time Ehrler had already received the *Eichenlaub* for 112 victories on August 2, 1943. Also of interest is the 100th victory marking with the date June 8, 1943. The victim was a Hawker Typhoon, an aircraft not seen in that far north.

Left: Hauptmann Ehrler, beside his "Yellow 12" of 6. JG 5, displaying the *Ritterkreuz* which he received on September 4, 1942 for over sixty-four victories. Ehrler lost his life on April 4, 1945 when for reasons unknown he rammed a B-17, his 208th and last victim.

A widely published aircraft is this "Yellow 12" of Heinrich Ehrler, here for the first time without winter camouflage.

The photos above, right, and center right show from left to right: Schuck, Dörr, Ehrler and Norz , in front of a Bf 109G with spiral spinner. These four *experten* had between them over 600 victories in the far north, and together with Weissenberger were the most successful pilots of JG 5.

As young student pilots from left to right: Martin Villing, Franz Josef Beerenbrock, Emil Stratmann and Hans Becker at Stolp-Reitz in 1940, posing in front of a Bf109C. Beerenbrock would later become a famous JG 51 pilot while the others flew with JG 5.

Martin Villing sittining in a Bf 109C-DH-19 during his pilot training days at Stolp-Reitz in 1940.

A Bf 109C-DH-19, with yellow fuselage tail band.

Pilots of JG 5 wearing the old style life jacket. *Fw* Villing is standing second from the left.

Pilots of the 10./JG 5 take time out for a snowball fight at Gossen airfield, Norway. From left to right are: *Fw* Wollmann, *Ofw* Villing, unknown, *Uffz* Reber and another unknown pilot. The aircraft in the background is a Bf 109G, "Black 4", with IV. *Gruppe* chevron. Note the tail section is white while victory markings are not.

Martin Villing sitting on his Bf 109G 6.

Fw Rudolf Müller of 6./II./JG 5 at home on holiday.

The winter camouflage of Bf 109G-2/R6 "Yellow 3" was often incorrectly published as Ehrlers aircraft. However, it was flown by Rudolf Müller, another ace of 6./JG 5, with a total of ninety-four victories.

Generaloberst Stumpf talking to the pilots of 6./JG 5. For the moment he is talking with Heinrich Ehrler, second from left. Also present was Rudolf Müller, first in the row, who had just received the *Ritterkreuz* as *Feldwebel* for his 41st victory on June 19, 1942.

Right: Müller made an emergency landing on Lake Bolschoje, near Murmansk on April 19, 1943, after a dogfight. He was awarded the *Ritterkreuz* on June 19, 1942 for forty-six victories, and as an *Ofw* was shot down and later died in a Russian prison, around 1947.

Above: Martin Ullmann sitting in *Ofw* Orlowski's Fw 190, "White 3", of 9./JG 5. The aircraft with the name "Ingeborg", after Ullmann's wife, is also marked with the IV. *Gruppe* chevron.

Right: *Uffz* Eisermann with one of his mechanics on his Fw 190A-3, Netty, at Herdla in early 1945.

Below: Heinrich Bartels of 8./JG 5 being presented with a plaque to commemorate his 100th combat mission on September 11, 1942. His Bf 109F, "Black 13", was named Hella. Bartels left JG 5 during the spring of 1943 with a total of forty-seven victories.

Left and below: Bf 109F, "Black 4", of 8./JG 5. This aircraft, with its unusual camouflage, belonged to *Ofw* Karl Schulz. The dark upper surface is oversprayed with white lines in an irregular manner. It was shot down by a Soviet fighter and overturned during the ensuing crash-landing.

This Bf 109F, "Black 3" of 8./JG 5 had the Staffel badge painted ahead of the Gruppe emblem. It is suggested that this was probably the machine of *Oblt* Hermann Seegatz, the unit's first *Staffelkapitän* until September 1943.

***Oberleutnant* Horst Berger in his Bf 109F, "Black 14." He took over 8./JG 5 after the departure of Seegatz.**

Bf 109E of *Hauptmann* Günther Scholz, *Gruppenkommandeur* of III/JG 5. The aircraft had a dark upperside camouflage and a white rudder that displayed thirty victories. Under the cockpit was the insignia of III/JG 5 along with Scholz's personal emblem, a rear view of a young woman in shorts.

Above: *Hptm* Günther Scholz with his Bf 109E. He was *Gruppenkommodeur* of the III./JG 5, from January 1942 to June 1943, and then as *Oberstlt* was *Geschwaderkommodore* from June 1943 to May 1944. Below: Rear view of Major Scholz's Bf 109F, of III./JG 5.

"Yellow 1" and "Yellow 3" of 7./JG 5 at Bodö, Norway during the winter of 1941-42. "Yellow 1" was the aircraft of *Staffelkapitän Hauptmann* Graf von Sponeck who also used the emblem while in his former unit.

Beautiful view of a Bf 109F, "Red 1", with the *Staffelkapitän, Uffz* Philipp, about to take off. This aircraft carried the standard grey camouflage scheme and the 7./JG 5 shield emblem, probably in red, black and white, under the cockpit. In each corner of the unit marking was a white diamond.

Standing in front of this Bf 109G-3/R6, "Yellow 10", is Hans Döbrich on the left and Albert Brunner on the right, of 6./ JG 5. Both men received the *Ritterkreuz* , Döbrich for a total of sixty-five victories, and Brunner fifty-three.

***Ltn* Heinicke's aircraft, a Bf 109G 6 of 7./JG 5, "Black 12", after a belly-landing on October 17, 1944. He had been hit but managed to bring it in safely to Kirkenes. One week later the airfield was destroyed during a retreat.**

The photographs on the left and right are of *Oblt* Rudolf Glöckner, another successful fighter pilot, with thirty-two victories, sitting on *Oblt* Dörr's Bf 109G-6. The center photograph shows Glöckner, in the middle, flanked by *Ltn* Gayko, on his left and *Oblt* Dörr to his right.

A group of JG 5 pilots with a Bf 109G-6/trop in unusual camouflage, possibly dark grey 74 and pale blue-grey 76 or white. It is believed to have carried a IV. *Gruppe* marking.

The same aircraft as above pictured with another group of pilots. Gayko and Amend are among them.

A front view of a Bf 109G, with the pilot Gayko on the right, who had a total of 13 victories.

Bf 109G of JG 5, standing in front from left to right: Müller, Steinbach, Klante, Bert and Senoner. The others are unknown.

"Staffel" dog at the propeller hood of a Bf 109G. This is identified by the two additional air scoops.

A group of mechanics and one pilot (the man wearing the light pants) standing in front of a Bf 109F.

Above: This photograph is of a Bf 109E, "Yellow 4", of 7./JG 5, as seen by the emblem. The pilot is unknown. This aircraft was formerly used by 1 (Einsatz)/Erg. *Jagdgruppe* 3 Esbjerg.

Right and top right: Mechanics with their Bf 109E of 7./JG 5 in Bodö.

Shoveling winters treasures was also the chore of the "Black men." Pictured in the background is "Yellow 7" of 7./JG 5.

Bf 109E landing.

The five photographs to the left and below are all of "Yellow 8", a Bf 109E. They were taken in Bodö during the winter of 1941-42.

Fw 190A-8s of 9./JG 5 at Herdla, Norway, in May 1945. The first machine was coded "Blue 8" and had the *Geschwader* emblem on its cowling, plus a IV. *Gruppe* marking on the rear fuselage.

"Yellow 6" a Bf 109E of 7./JG 5, over Norway during the winter of 1941-42.

This was the kind of terrain over which JG 5 fought its icy war. In the center of the photograph are two Bf 109s.

Above: This was the enemy – a pair of I-16s.

Right: A pair of Russian Hurricanes over Nautsi, Finland.

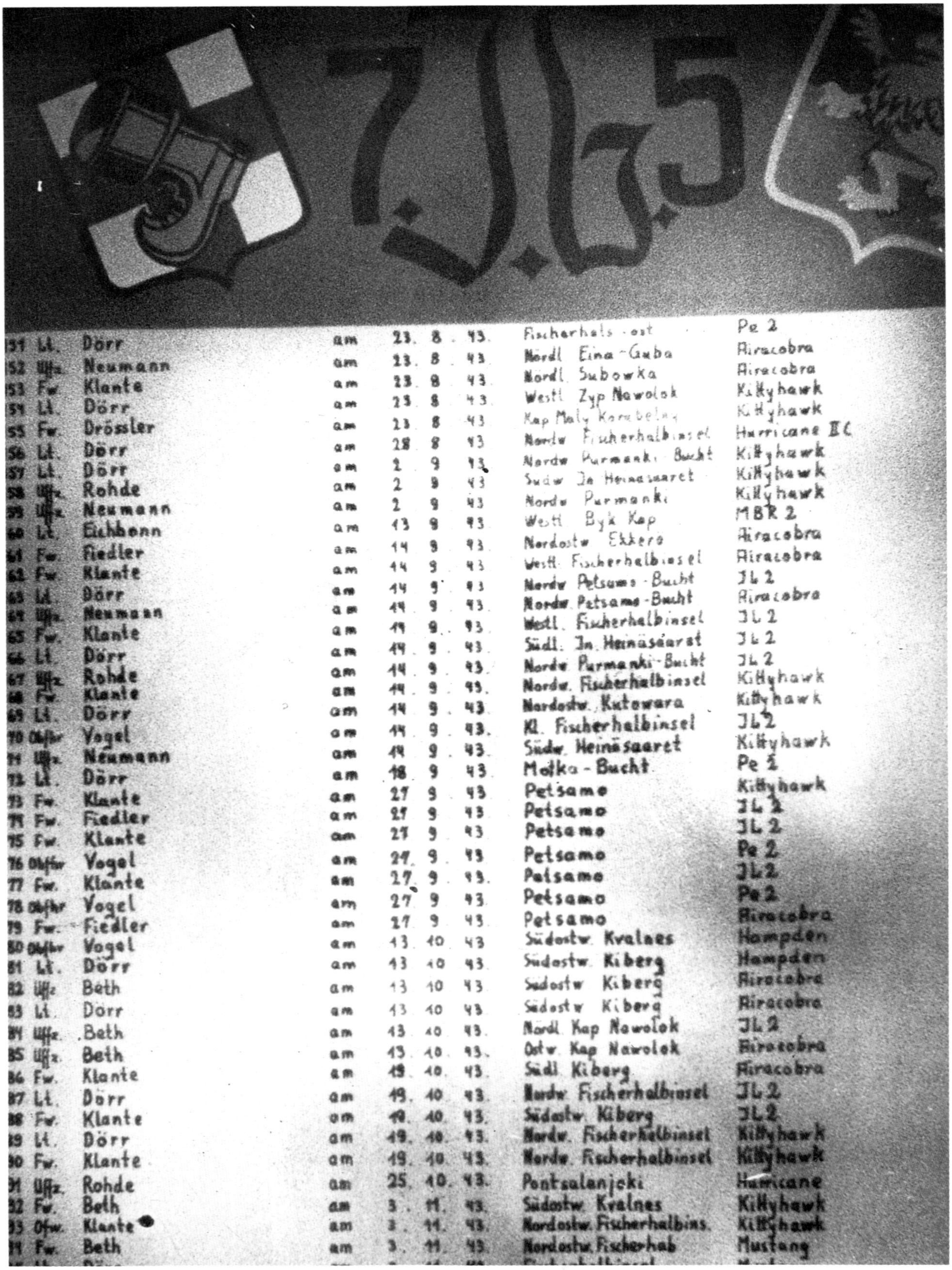

No.	Rank	Name		Date	Location	Aircraft
151	Lt.	Dörr	am	23. 8. 43.	Fischerhals-ost	Pe 2
152	Uffz.	Neumann	am	23. 8. 43.	Nördl. Eina-Guba	Airacobra
153	Fw.	Klante	am	23. 8. 43.	Nördl. Subowka	Airacobra
154	Lt.	Dörr	am	23. 8. 43.	Westl. Zyp Nawolok	Kittyhawk
155	Fw.	Drössler	am	23. 8. 43.	Kap Maly Korabelny	Kittyhawk
156	Lt.	Dörr	am	28. 8. 43.	Nordw. Fischerhalbinsel	Hurricane IIC
157	Lt.	Dörr	am	2. 9. 43.	Nordw. Purmanki-Bucht	Kittyhawk
158	Uffz.	Rohde	am	2. 9. 43.	Südw. In. Heinäsaaret	Kittyhawk
159	Uffz.	Neumann	am	2. 9. 43.	Nordw. Purmanki	Kittyhawk
60	Lt.	Eichhorn	am	13. 9. 43.	Westl. Byk Kap	MBR 2
61	Fw.	Fiedler	am	14. 9. 43.	Nordostw. Ekkerö	Airacobra
62	Fw.	Klante	am	14. 9. 43.	Westl. Fischerhalbinsel	Airacobra
63	Lt.	Dörr	am	14. 9. 43.	Nordw. Petsamo-Bucht	IL 2
64	Uffz.	Neumann	am	14. 9. 43.	Nordw. Petsamo-Bucht	Airacobra
65	Fw.	Klante	am	14. 9. 43.	Westl. Fischerhalbinsel	IL 2
66	Lt.	Dörr	am	14. 9. 43.	Südl. In. Heinäsaaret	IL 2
67	Uffz.	Rohde	am	14. 9. 43.	Nordw. Purmanki-Bucht	IL 2
68	Fw.	Klante	am	14. 9. 43.	Nordw. Fischerhalbinsel	Kittyhawk
69	Lt.	Dörr	am	14. 9. 43.	Nordostw. Kutowara	Kittyhawk
70	Obfhr.	Vogel	am	14. 9. 43.	Kl. Fischerhalbinsel	IL 2
71	Uffz.	Neumann	am	14. 9. 43.	Südw. Heinäsaaret	Kittyhawk
72	Lt.	Dörr	am	18. 9. 43.	Motka-Bucht	Pe 2
73	Fw.	Klante	am	27. 9. 43.	Petsamo	Kittyhawk
74	Fw.	Fiedler	am	27. 9. 43.	Petsamo	IL 2
75	Fw.	Klante	am	27. 9. 43.	Petsamo	IL 2
76	Obfhr.	Vogel	am	27. 9. 43.	Petsamo	Pe 2
77	Fw.	Klante	am	27. 9. 43.	Petsamo	IL 2
78	Obfhr.	Vogel	am	27. 9. 43.	Petsamo	Pe 2
79	Fw.	Fiedler	am	27. 9. 43.	Petsamo	Airacobra
80	Obfhr.	Vogel	am	13. 10. 43.	Südostw. Kvalnes	Hampden
81	Lt.	Dörr	am	13. 10. 43.	Südostw. Kiberg	Hampden
82	Uffz.	Beth	am	13. 10. 43.	Südostw. Kiberg	Airacobra
83	Lt.	Dörr	am	13. 10. 43.	Südostw. Kiberg	Airacobra
84	Uffz.	Beth	am	13. 10. 43.	Nördl. Kap Nawolok	IL 2
85	Uffz.	Beth	am	13. 10. 43.	Ostw. Kap Nawolok	Airacobra
86	Fw.	Klante	am	19. 10. 43.	Südl. Kiberg	Airacobra
87	Lt.	Dörr	am	19. 10. 43.	Nordw. Fischerhalbinsel	IL 2
88	Fw.	Klante	am	19. 10. 43.	Südostw. Kiberg	IL 2
89	Lt.	Dörr	am	19. 10. 43.	Nordw. Fischerhalbinsel	Kittyhawk
90	Fw.	Klante	am	19. 10. 43.	Nordw. Fischerhalbinsel	Kittyhawk
91	Uffz.	Rohde	am	25. 10. 43.	Pontsalenjoki	Hurricane
92	Fw.	Beth	am	3. 11. 43.	Südostw. Kvalnes	Kittyhawk
93	Ofw.	Klante	am	3. 11. 43.	Nordostw. Fischerhalbins.	Kittyhawk
94	Fw.	Beth	am	3. 11. 43.	Nordostw. Fischerhalb.	Mustang

Victory list of 7./JG 5, showing victories 131 through 200.

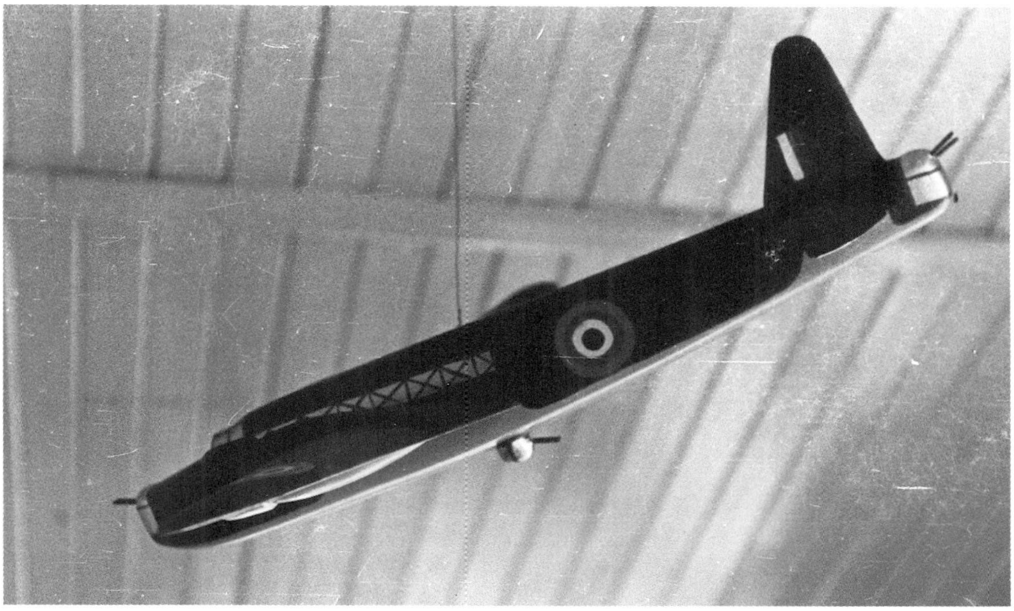

A model of the Wellington

A model of the Do 215

A model of the Hs 136

Maj Gerhard Barkhorn, wearing his battle honors. As *Hauptmann*, he was decorated, on March 2, 1944 with the *"Ritterkreuz mit Eichenlaub und Schwertern"*, for 250 victories. On January 16, 1945 he became *Kommodore* of JG 6.

Chapter 6

JAGDGESCHWADER 6 "HORST WESSEL"

Although this unit only operated for a short time, it nevertheless had a colorful history. In August and September 1944, JG 6 was formed from the *Geschwaderstab* and both the first and second *Gruppen* of ZG 26, a bomber-destroyer unit.

On August 20, 1944, II./JG 6 moved to a location near Reims in France, but within a few days of intense fighting was almost wiped out. The following month the *Geschwaderstab* and I. *Gruppe* moved to airfields in the Bonn area. In October a third *Gruppe* was added, having previously been I./JG 5. In November the entire *Geschwader* saw action from airfields to the east of Mecklenburg, moving in December to a base near Oldenburg.

For JG 6, Operation *Bodenplatte* was a complete disaster. At the time, I./JG 6 was based at Delmenhorst with II./JG 6 at Vechta and III./JG 6 at Bissel. In the early morning about 70 aircraft, Bf 109G-10s and G-14s plus a few Fw 190A-8s and A-9s, took off to assemble over Quakenbrück. Flying low at about 150 meters, they proceeded west but missed their turning point and mistakenly attacked Heesch, where Spitfires of the 126th Wing of the 2nd Tactical Air Force were based. Attacks were also made on Twenthe and Venlo, but only one air victory was claimed for a devastating loss of 23 pilots.

Shortly afterward, the entire *Geschwader* moved to the Posen area on the Eastern Front, III. *Gruppe* then proceeding to Oberschlesien. Commencing from January 1945, ground attack missions were mounted against the overwhelming might of the Russian advance in the Niederlausitz sector, but starved of fuel and after losing many ground personnel to the army, the unit gradually disintegrated. A retreat to Prague followed. Finally, what was left of JG 6 surrendered after reaching Bavaria.

Gerhard Barkhorn *Kommodore* of JG 6, with his Fw 190D-9 named *Christl*, and his mechanic Albert Kusterer in February 1945.

Barkhorn and comrades in front of the wing of an unidentified Fw 190D-9. The dark 81 and 82 camouflage is obvious as are the white "Don't Walk" markings.

Barkhorn in his Fw 190D-9 on February 17, 1945 in Welzow, Niederlausitz. Note the MW 50 markings.

Above: Barkhorn climbing out of his Fw 190D-9. Note the tiny "White 5" behind the chevron and the name Christl, Barkhorn's wife. Both markings dated from his first Bf 109F, "White 5", which he flew at the start of the Russian campaign.

Left: General Deßloch together with Barkhorn during an inspection of JG 6. Note the covered Fw 190D-9 in the background and on the right a Bf 109K-4, that was also used by Barkhorn.

Barkhorn looking at his watch, waiting for action. Notice the load-markings on the main wheel strut cover, and that the Balkenkreuz on the underwing is outlined in black.

Once again *General* Deßloch, on the left, and Barkhorn with a Fw 190D-9 in the background with a white spiral around the black spinner.

Below: *Major* Barkhorn, second from the left flanked by his comrades, including his *Katschmarek, Fähnrich* Graf Keller.

Me 262, "White 13", W Nr 110522 of III./EJG 2, in the Spring of 1945 at Lechfeld.

Me 262 "Yellow 10" during a landing. This aircraft probably belonged to *Erprobungskommando* 262.

Chapter 7

JAGDGESCHWADER 7 "NOWOTNY"

The nucleus of JG 7 was the *Kommando Nowotny,* which had been established in the summer of 1944 by the *General der Jagdflieger*, Adolf Galland. Further personnel came from *Erprobungskommando Lechfeld,* which in turn had been formed from III./ZG 26.

The first missions, from Lärz, Hesepe and Achmer met with only marginal success, for the defenders' airspace was on the direct bomber route to Berlin. Toward the end of November 1944, the unit was placed under the command of the *Geschwaderstab* of JG 7 in the Berlin area, thus forming III. *Gruppe*. I. *Gruppe* was established from former members of II./JG 3 and operated from Neumünster/Kaltenkirchen, until the final month of the war, when large numbers of miscellaneous fighter and bomber pilots were transferred in. The unit took no part in the *Bodenplatte* operation.

II. *Gruppe* reached operational readiness in February 1945 and together with the *Stabsschwarm*, which consisted of *Experten* from JG 5 and I. *Gruppe*, achieved very good results against Allied bomber streams and their escorting fighters.

It is not clear how many victories were achieved by JG 7, but it is believed to have been close to 500. The last of these was also the last WW 2 air-to-air victory in the European theatre, when *Oblt* Stehle and his wingman shot down a Russian Yak 9 near Freiberg on May 8, 1945.

An Me 262A-1a, "White 7", acting as an interceptor in 1945.

***Hptm* Franz Schall with his Me 262, "White 1", of JG 7, and his mechanic. Schall had a total of 133 victories, sixteen he acquired with this Me 262. He was killed, after his last victory on April 10, 1945, when he made an emergency landing at Parchim airfield and hit a bomb crater causing the aircraft to explode.**

American soldier checking out the remains of an Me 262.

A front view of an Me 262 found at an assembly point by U.S. forces after the capitulation.

Jumo engines belonging to the Me 262s. In the background is a Ta 154.

Me 262, W Nr 170067, "Yellow 3" of *Erprobungskommando* 262, at Lechfeld in July 1944.

Me 262V-3, W Nr 26200003, prototype, tested at Leipheim in July 1942. In the background a Messerschmitt Me 321 "Gigant" is visible.

A rear view of the same machine. Engine control, just before takeoff.

Another view of the Me 262V-3, W Nr 26200003, prototype.

Me 262s of *Erprobungskommando* 262, probably at Lechfeld in July 1944. The second aircraft was "Yellow 3", W NR 170067, but its camouflage, as with all the aircraft here, is a moot point.

An *Adjutants* Me 262, "Red 3," Chevron of the III./JG 7. Note the two 21cm launch tubes.

On March 30, 1945, Messerschmitt test pilot Hans Fay surrendered this prize Me 262, W Nr 111711, to the USAAF, making it the first intact German jet to fall into Allied hands. Toward the end of the war production difficulties resulted in many aircraft being flown with only part-finished paintwork.

Me 262 with overpainted Swastika.

Another Me 262.

Large parts of this abondoned Me 262-1b appear to thave been painted with a light color, others seem to have been primed and yet others left in natural metal, a very interesting combination which probably came about because of disruptions to production in the final weeks of war.

Me 262 damaged by a bomb blast, found by advancing Allied forces in 1945. Such sights were common on many airfields.

This Me 262A-1a interceptor, W Nr 501232, "Yellow 5", is believed to have been decorated with a tail band consisting of blue and green checks. It belonged to 3./ISS 1, a special factory defense unit based at Lechfeld. Standing on the left is USAAF officer Colonel Watson.

An Me 262A-2a, KG51.

The remains of an He 162 near Viennna, Austria.

The charred and twisted remains of this Me 262 which crashed on April 18, 1945 in München-Reim. The pilot, *Obst* Johannes Steinhoff, miraculously survived but suffered serious burns. At that time his tally stood at 176 confirmed victories.

Above: The remains of an He 162A-1.

Right: An He 162 destroyed while sitting in a hangar.

The remains of He 162, W Nr 220003, "M20."

He 162, W Nr 220006, M23, "VI+IP." "M20" is in the background.

"White 23", W Nr 120222, was the identification of this He 162A-2. It had the basic color scheme of 71/76, due to the need to use up surplus paint stocks as sent out in the painting directives of July 1, 1944, when three new green shades were introduced.

Pilots of JG 11 sitting in the grass near the airfield during March 1944. From left to right: *Ofhr* Dreizehner, *Olt* Koenig, *Olt* Zwernemann, *Lt* Schrangl, and Rolf Hermichen, *Kommandeur* of I/JG 11 with *Ritterkreuz*. In the background Rolf Hermichen can be seen to the left and Otto Heinzmann on the right.

Opposite: Pilots of 3./JG 11. From right to left stands Heinz Stöwer, Günthenke and Hanke.

Chapter 8

JAGDGESCHWADER 11

During April 1943, a completely new fighter *Geschwader* was formed for home defense purposes, using elements of JG 1 for its establishment. The *Geschwaderstab* was based at Jever. I./JG 11, formed from III./JG 1, was based at Husum and II./JG 11, formed from I./JG 1, was based at Rheine. A short time later, III. *Gruppe* was established at Neumünster and this unit moved to Oldenburg. At the same time and in the same area of Northwestern Germany, there was an autonomous fighter unit operating under the designation *Jagdstaffel Helgoland* which later became 11./JG 11. They were joined by a newly formed tenth *Staffel* from Aalborg in Denmark.

After operating for a short spell in Norway, I./JG 11 rejoined the rest of the *Geschwader* on home defense duties, but a fighter pilot's life was not easy in those days when the American daylight offensive was at its height and the unit suffered heavy losses. Even heavier were the losses in France after D-Day, when I., II., and IV. *Gruppen* operated against the invasion forces from bases north of Paris. II./JG 11, flying Bf 109's. was withdrawn to Wunstorf to rest and refit, but by August returned to the battle for Northern France. Meanwhile, III./JG 11 had moved to the Eastern Front, to fight over the central and northern sectors until moving back to Germany in September 1944.

The first three *Gruppen* took part in the great New Year's Day attack on the Allied airfields. Under the *Kommodore, Major* Günther Specht, they took off from bases south of Frankfurt and set course for Asch in Belgium. The attack was a failure and 25 pilots were lost including the *Kommodore* and *Hauptmann* von Fassong, *Gruppenkommandeur* of III./JG 11. During the latter part of January the unit moved to the Posen area and took part in the Battle for Berlin in February. During March, I. *Gruppe* was disbanded and II. *Gruppe* disappeared. What remained of JG 11 was found at the time of the capitulation in Schleswig-Holstein and in Denmark and Norway.

Anton Hackl, *Gruppenkommandeur* of III./JG 11, in his grey Fw 190 which had a roaring dragon for the pilot's personal emblem.

A victory bar is being added to the same machine, for Hackl's 141st, accomplished on April 11, 1944. It had the yellow tail band of JG 11, a III. *Gruppe* bar and an oversprayed swastika.

Anton Hackl, center, with two companions in front of his grey-camouflaged Bf 109G-6. It had a yellow rear fuselage band, III. *Gruppe* bar and featured 132 victories on its white rudder. Hackl used this machine in parallel with a Fw 190, the former for combat against opposing escort fighters and the latter for attacking bombers.

Two *Kommodores* of JG 11: on the left is Anton Hackl and on the right, Anton Mader.

Major Günther Specht with his *Ritterkreuz.*

The decorated aircraft, Bf 109G-5AS, of *Major* Günther Specht *Gruppenkommandeur* of II./JG11. The honor took place on April 8, 1944, when Specht received the *Ritterkreuz* for thirty-one victories.

A close-up of the *Ritterkreuz* on *Maj* Spechts aircraft.

***Leutnant* Günther Specht parading with comrades in 1939.**

Hauptmann Clausen, of the I./JG 11, on September 4, 1943 after receiving the *Ritterkreuz.*

Maj Erwin Clausen's rudder showing 129 victories. On October 4, 1943, when as *Gruppenkommandeur* of I./JG 11, he was killed in action over the North Sea. His total at that time stood at 132.

Left: This shot of Hans König in the cockpit of his Fw 190 was taken in Rotenburg.

Below: Hans Heinrich "Kira" König, *Staffelkapitän* of 3./JG 11 in front of his Fw 190, W Nr 430689. The rudder shows a total of seventeen victories, two British and fifteen American.

These two photographs are of Hans König before his untimely death. He was killed in action when his last target exploded taking his Fw 190 with it. He was later awarded the *Ritterkreuz* for a total of twenty-four victories.

Hans König with the fiancée of "Heino" Hanke in front of Fw 190, W Nr 430682.

Hans König once again with the fiancée of "Heino" Hanke. König's Fw 190, "Yellow 4", is visible in the background.

Hans König saluting *Gen* Stumpff in Rotenburg on April 2, 1944. Note very pale colored Fw 190 in the background.

Hans König pictured with the "Black Men" of JG 11.

Two young women standing in front of Hans König's Fw 190, "Yellow 4."

Hans Georg Güthenke climbing out of his Fw 190 after marking his first victory, a P-38 Lightning, on June 11, 1943. He is being greeted and congratulated by his mechanic "Rudi."

On June 26, 1943 Günthenke had again scored a victory as seen in this rudder shot of his Fw 190, W Nr 530106.

Oberleutnant Strobl congratulates Hans Günthenke, of 3./JG 11, with a champagne toast.

With his Fw 190 behind him Günthenke sips his champaign while being congratulated by his fellow comrades on his first victory.

General Stumpff awarding the *EK 1* (iron cross) to Georg Güthenke, during April of 1944 in Rotenburg. Standing to the left of Güthenke is "Heino" Hanke, and Rudi Schmitt to his right. Standing behind Stumpff is *General* Ibel.

Hans Günthenke's Fw 190A-6, "Yellow" 7, W Nr 530106, at Husum in 1943. The 3./JG 11 badge is just visible on the cowling.

On August 17, 1943 Günthenke had to make an emergency landing between Zutphen and Arnheim, causing him to miss the interception of the huge Schweinfurt-Regensberg raid. At this time he about five victories displayed on his "Yellow 7's" rudder.

Left: Hans Leyer, Günthenke's mechanic, standing in front of "Yellow 7's" rudder, in June of 1943.

Below: An Fw 190 on the wooden airstip at Husum.

Above: "Heino" Heinz Hanke, of 3./JG 11, in his Fw 190 "Yellow 2."

Right: Heinz Hanke standing in front of Lorenz's "Yellow 15" which also carried the 3./JG 11 emblem on the hood.

Heinz Hanke in front of a Fw 190 that displays the 3./JG 11 emblem on the hood.

Heinz Hanke in front of a Fw 190.

"Yellow 11" with Born and Hanke.

Heinz Born is welcomed home with champagne by Heinz Hanke, on the left, just after he shot down a Spitfire in "Yellow 11", an Fw 190A-3.

The two photos above are of Lorenz's Fw 190, "Yellow 15", being worked on inside a hangar.

Lorenz standing beside his "Yellow 15" an Fw 190 (probably an A-7 type).

Uffz Kabus in his Fw 190F-8, "Yellow 7", in Straussberg during March of 1945. He is carrying an AB 250 small bomb container loaded with 108 SD-2 bombs. These were used against unarmored targets.

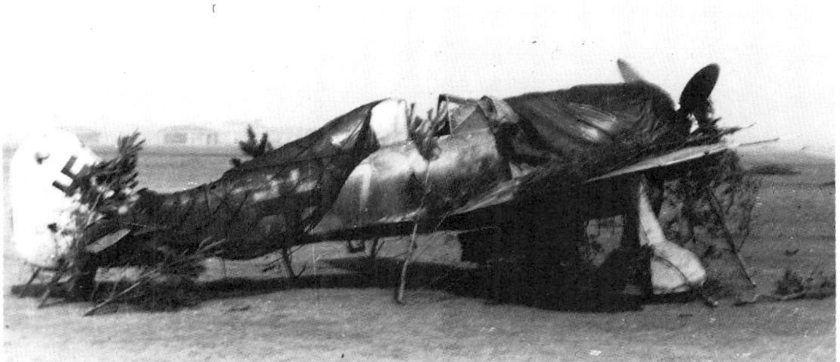

Fw 190F-8, "Yellow 7", of *Uffz* Kabus photographed while at Straussberg, near Berlin, during March of 1945.

Günther Wiemann's crash at Husum on March 3, 1943.

Günther "Matthias" Wiemann in his Fw 190 before his fatal crash on May 20, 1944.

Otto Heinzmann, on the left, with his mechanic in front of his Fw 190A-7/MK in Rothenburg during 1944.

Heinzmann in his Fw 190, showing interesting close-up details.

Otto Heinzmann, of I./JG 11, in front of his Fw 190A-7/MK.

Otto Heinzmann, third from the left, with his comrades at JG 107 school, in Nancy, France.

***Uffz* Herman Hoes, on the left, with Gutowski, the *Staffelkapitän*, at Husum in 1942. In the background is Gutowski's "Yellow 1", displaying the 3./ JG 11 emblem, located on the fuselage, just behind the *Balkenkreuz*.**

Ltn Heinert, of 3./ JG 11, in front of his Fw 190 "Yellow 13." He died on October 9, 1943.

Rudi Schmitt in front of a late-model Fw 190 fitted with four additional guns in the underwing gondolas. He was killed over Normandy in July 1944.

Herrmann Jäger standing beside his Fw 190.

Ltn **Alwin Doppler in his Fw 190. On January 1, 1945 he was reported missing in action over Asch, Belgium.**

This Fw 190A-7/MK, "Black 1" of 2./JG 11, was fitted with two 30mm MK 108 cannon and was normally flown by either Zwernemann or Doppler.

The photographs above and to the right are of *Fw* Allan Gödicke of 3./JG 11. Above he is with his Fw 190. He was killed in action on February 10, 1944 in Rheine.

Heinz Stöwer, of 3/JG 11, in the cockpit of his Fw 190. He died on May 30, 1944.

Rolf Hermichen, standing on the right, received the Ritterkreuz on March 26, 1944 for approximately fifty victories. Here he is being toasted, from left to right, by: Dreizehner, König, Jan Stangl and Stöwer.

Right: An unidentified pilot of 3./*Staffel* with "Yellow 14", which featured an unusually solid style of camouflage on its fuselage sides.

Two Fw 190s at Rothenburg, "Black 13" in the background.

These seven aircraft of 3./JG 11 were photographed at Husum, and by this time were all carrying wide yellow rear fuselage bands.

An unusual close-up view of the nose of a 3. *Staffel* Fw 190 at Rottenburg showing its gun and heart unit emblem and "pulk-destroyer" armament.

An Fw 190 with overpainted markings as this was often the only way to get home safely.

A low flying Fw 190 of the I./JG 11 somewhere over North Germany.

These two aircraft of 3./JG 11 had been fitted with auxiliary fuel tanks. With their markings overpainted they were much more difficult to spot at low level.

This Fw 190 of 3./JG 11 was photographed during 1943 while under repair on the wooden strip at Husum.

The strip and dispersal areas at Husum was so muddy that boards had to be used to prevent the aircraft from being bogged down. This 1943 shot shows a typical scene. All of the aircraft had white borders to their fuselage crosses and narrow white rear fuselage bands

Right: In these three photographs we see quite a few Fw 190s of I./ JG 11 during an emergency take-off from Rotenburg. The use of pine boards for taxiways was very unusual.

The devastating effects of an Allied bombing raid are seen in this dramatic shot of burning Fw 190s of JG 11.

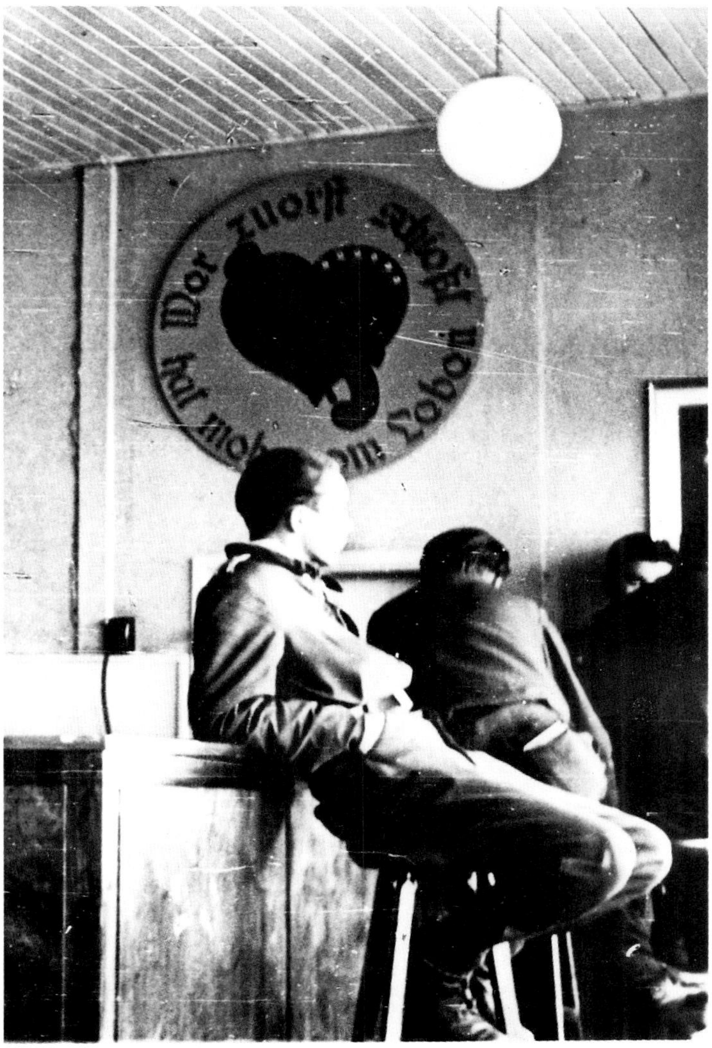

In the 3./JG 11 mess was a large replica of the unit's gun and heart emblem surrounded by the words: "Wer zuerst schiesst hat mehr von Leben" ("He who shoots first lives longest").

" After the mission."

One of our pilots is missing . . . a photograph which speaks eloquently of the tragedy of total war, whatever the nationality of the airmen.

Adolf Galland as *Kommodore* of JG 26, showing *"Ritterkreuz with Eichenlaub and Schwertern."*

Adolf Galland as *Oberst,* showing the "Brillianten."

Chapter 9

JAGDGESCHWADER 26 "SCHLAGETER"

Only I. and II. *Gruppe* existed at the outbreak of WWII, and III. *Gruppe* was established soon afterward. The entire *Geschwader* remained in the West until it was called upon to take part in the French campaign and then in the Battle of Britain. In April 1941, JG 26 withdrew briefly to Germany, from where 7. *Staffel* moved to Sicily to operate over Malta, while the rest of the unit returned to France, occupying airfields in the St Omer region, their place in Germany being taken by JG 2. During the summer of 1941, JG 26 began to convert to the Fw 190 and in March 1942, 10. (Jabo)/JG 26 (a fighter-bomber *Staffel*) was established, equipped with Bf 109s and Fw 190s for attacking targets in Southern England and in the Channel. In February 1943, this *Staffel* was absorbed by a new unit, SKG 10. *(Schnellkampfgeschwader 10).* On 19th August 1942, JG 26 was heavily committed over Dieppe and claimed a large number of victories. During the same month, 11. *Staffel* was formed as a high-altitude unit, but in November it moved to the Mediterranean area and became a part of JG 51. In JG 26 a new 11. *Staffel* was formed, followed in April 1943 by 12. *Staffel.* The *Geschwader* continued operations over France, moving to the Paris area after D-Day and to the Netherlands at the end of August 1944. The sustained heavy fighting in the air continued and by the end of 1944 JG 26 had been forced to withdraw into Germany, to airfields around Rheine.

On the great attack of New Year's Day 1945, JG 26 took off with III./JG 54 (later to become part of JG 26) to attack Grimbergen and Evère, near Brussels. About 180 aircraft were involved, mainly Fw 190D-9s, and at Evère they succeeded in destroying about 120 Allied aircraft on the ground, including most of the Spitfires of 416 Sqn RAF. During the closing months of the war, JG 26 moved further back into Northern Germany and surrendered there in May.

Adolf Galland with his officers waiting for the *Führer* one day before Christmas 1940 at Chateau Bonnance in Abbeville. In the background from left: Schöpfel, Adolf and Pingl, the three *Gruppenkommandeure* of JG 26.

Adolf Galland climbing out of his Bf 109E, already *Kommodore* of JG 26. Aircraft is showing a JG 26 emblem and as a special feature, ZFR 5 telescopic sight.

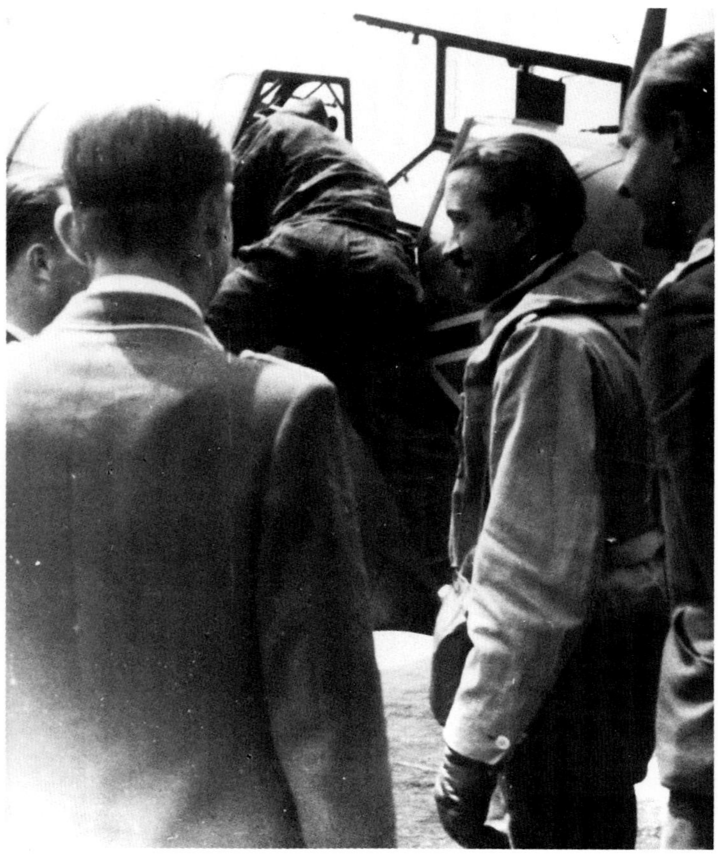

As above, with *Hauptmann* Ewald on the left side foreground.

Bf 109E-4, W Nr was 5819, of Adolf Galland showing *Kommodore* markings. At this time, December 1940, he had about fifty-seven victories. Airfield was Audembert, France.

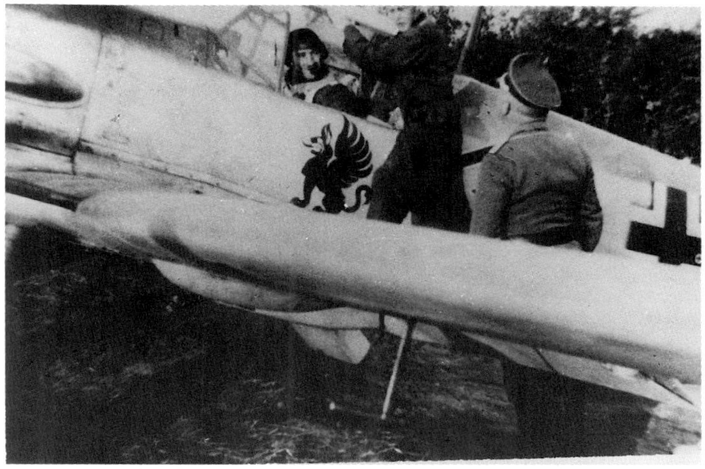

This Bf 109E, shown with Galland in the cockpit, carries the markings of the *Gruppenkommandeur of* III./JG 26. On the aircraft was the red *Höllenhund* badge of 9. *Staffel.*

Adolf Galland in front of a *Kommodore* Bf 109.

Galland (left) with comrades and brother "Wutz."

A further shot of Bf 109E-4, W Nr 5819, which carried the markings of a *Kommodore* and a tally of fifty-seven victories on its yellow rudder.

Galland again but in a different aircraft which bore the "Mickey Mouse" marking facing aft. The special telescopic sight was used for identifying enemy aircraft, not for aerial gunnery.

Werner Mölders visiting Galland in Wissant during September 1940. On the left, Galland's adjutant, *Oberleutnant* Rotenberger.

A complete view of the machine shown in the photograph above, taken in December 1940 at Audembert in the Pas de Calais.

Center right: Galland and Meinardus in Audembert, France, during August of 1941.

Right: Galland is looking at the rudder of a Bf 109E. Rudder is showing five victories, and belonged to the aircraft of the *Geschwader* technical officer.

Rudder of Galland's Bf 109E showing fifty-five victories, around December 1940.

Reichsmarschall **Hermann Göring chats to Galland, by which time Galland had achieved ninety-five victories.**

Above: A close-up of rudder showing Gallands ninety-five victories.

Left: Rudder of Gallands Bf 109 showing seventy-three or seventy-four victories, around September 1941.

The two photographs above show Galland with *Reichsmarschall* Hermann Göring during an inspection tour in December 1941. The aircraft is one of two previously flown by the former pilot, its high-gloss finish being the result of special waxing and polishing. The photograph below shows the same grey-camouflaged Bf 109F-2 seen in the foreground as Göring addresses a parade of JG 26 members from the podium on the right. The aircraft had MG FF armament in the wing and a yellow rudder adorned with ninety-four victories.

The photographs on this and the next five pages show Galland throughout the 1941 period.

S

Oblt **Joachim Müncheberg,** ***Staffelkapitän*** ***of*** **7./JG 26, in the cockpit of a yellow-nosed Bf 109E-7 at Gela, Sicily, in 1941.**

Müncheberg's usual Bf 109E-7 in Sicily during 1941. Judging by the appearance around the cockpit, it was either a different aircraft to the one shown above or had been repainted.

Above: Joachim Mündeberg with *Eichenlaub* surrounded by pilots of his *staffel*. Second from the left is *Ofw*. Laube, while the pilot to the left beside Mündeberg is Mietusch.

Above: On the left, Müncheberg, with *adjutant* Lindemann, France, 1940.

Right: Müncheberg with friend, probably Galland's pet, *Schweine-bauch*. The *Eichenlaub* award can just be seen.

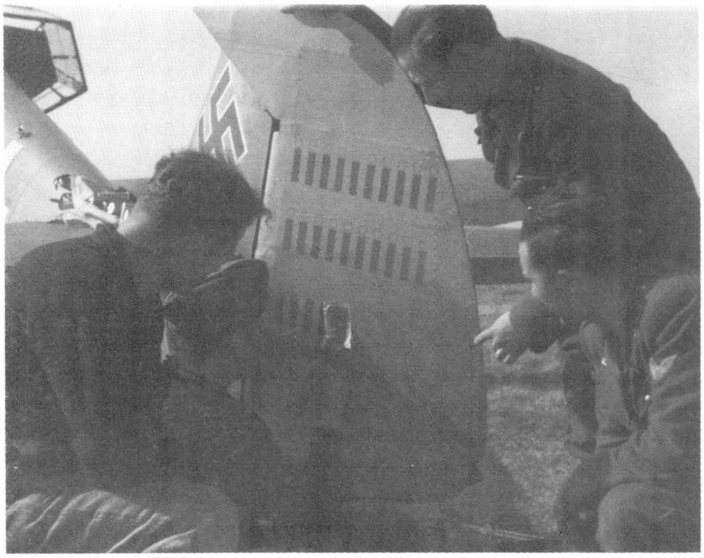

The last of twenty-five victories scored by Joachim Müncheberg being added to the yellow rudder of his Bf 109. The identity of this aircraft is not known.

The yellow rudder of Müncheberg's Fw 190 had a very detailed scoreboard and in early 1942 displayed sixty-five victories. At the time he was Gr*uppenkommandeur* of II./JG 26.

Oberleutnant Müncheberg with *Ritterkreuz*.

Major **Müncheberg 1943 in Bari, here already wearing the *"Schwerter"*, which he received on September 9, 1942 for 103 victories.**

Major **Müncheberg wearing the *"Schwerter."***

Member of PR film team filming newly arrived Fw 190s.

The same Fw 190A-1 of 5./JG 26, "Black 5"

Above: *Oberleutnant* Wolfgang Kosse, *Staffelkapitän* of 5./JG 26 in his Fw 190A-1, "Black 10."

Below: Kosse with comrades.

Above and left: A hint of the dramatic success of the newly introduced Fw 190 is provided in this shot of a Fw 190A-1, W Nr 027, "Yellow 1", of *Oblt* Walter Schneider in November 1941, which showed nineteen victory markings on its yellow rudder. The lower part of the cowling was also yellow. He was later killed in a crash.

Schneider on right.

Left: Mündeberg with white jacket talking to comrades.

Mündeberg and Laube dressed in track and field clothing.

Laube in front of his Bf 109E, note Gruppe bar in white.

Left: *Leutnant* Laube.

Fw 190A-1 flown by *Hpt* Ernst Laube in late 1941.

Lt Laube and his Bf 109E, "White 15", also of 7./JG 26.

Lt Laube in the cockpit of "White 3" in Sicily, its bright red heart emblem contrasting strongly with the pale yellow cowling.

Laube in cockpit of Bf 109.

Pilots of 7./JG 26. In the center is Laube.

Pilots of 7. *Staffel* in front of their Bf 109E-7s in Sicily. The nearest aircraft is "White 14."

Pilots of 7./JG 26 sitting on 300 litre fuel tanks. In the background is a Bf 110 of ZG 26.

Major Schöpfel with *Ritterkreuz.*

Maj Gerhard Schöpfel, the *Gruppenkommandeur* of III./JG 26, with his Fw 190. He was credited with forty-two victories.

Johannes Naumann of 8. *Staffel* prior to another mission in his Bf 109F. The cartoon figure, *Adamson,* was the emblem of 8./JG 26. Not long after this photograph was taken Naumann was awarded the *Ritterkreuz,* recording thirty-four victories in the West.

Right. Paul Galland, a brother of the better-known Adolf Galland, in a Bf 109F of the same *Staffel.*

This Bf 109F of 8./JG 26 carried an unusually small black number in conjunction with the III. *Gruppe* bar. The *Staffel* badge was painted under the cockpit.

Werner Bohnenkamp of 9./JG 26 in his Bf 109F at the end of 1940.

The red and white winged griffon emblem of 9./JG 26 on a Bf 109F.

An unidentified pilot of 9./JG 26 in his Bf 109F.

Georg Peter Eder with "Eichenlaub."

Eder, right, explaining a dogfight to his friend "Olaf." In the background a Bf 109G. He had a total of seventy-eight victories including thirty-six four-engine bobmbers.

Below: Bf 109E of JG 26.

Above: The introduction of the Fw 190 saw many scenes of jubilant pilots returning with stories of spectacular successes over the highly respected Spitfire. In the foreground is *Hpt* Stolle, *Staffelkapitän* of 8./JG 26 on November 26, 1942 when the unit had just made its 200th victory claim. Below: *Ofw* Glunz and his Fw 190. He had a total of seventy-one victories, including twenty four-engine bombers.

Glunz leaving his Fw 190.

Josef (Pips) Priller in front of his Bf 109F, evidently being congratulated on his latest victory.

An overhead camouflage net was responsible for the curious dappled appearance of this Fw 190 occupied by *Hpt* Josef Priller, who was credited with a final tally of 101 victories.

Above and below: Fw 190s at Marienehe, ready for transferring to JG 26.

Oberleutnant Priller, left, and *Oberfeldwebel* Glunz.

With "Black 10" in the background, two unidentified pilots of JG 26 discuss combat tactics.

A photograph taken on November 10, 1941 showing what the *Luftwaffe* so concisely called an *Alarmstart*. Movement of the starter motor crank handle required considerable effort.

Above and below: Bf 109E of JG 26, probably of 6th Staffel.

"Ruhe! Gefechtsalarm!"

Above and left: Bf 109 E of 6./JG 26. "Yellow 5" and "Yellow 8." Note W Nr 1935 at cockpit window of "Yellow 8."

This page and opposite: Various views of JG 26 markings.

Pilots of JG 27. On the left are *Lt* Gorny and *Lt* Börngen whilst third from the right was *Hpt* Lippert, the *Kommandeur,* and on the far right, *Lt* Doyé. The second aircraft, that of the *Gruppenadjudant* carried the II. *Gruppe* emblem on its cowling and a large caricature of a lion under the cockpit.

Chapter 10

JAGDGESCHWADER 27

The beginnings of JG 27 were to be found in 1939 when I./JG 1 became in effect, although not yet in its designation, the third *Gruppe* of the new unit. After the Polish operations, I. and II. *Gruppen* were formed and the entire *Geschwader* fought through the French campaign and the Battle of Britain. By November 1940, the unit was back in Germany preparing for the 1941 Balkan campaign, during which JG 27 remained in Romania and Bulgaria until the Greek capitulation. During the summer, III. *Gruppe* moved to Sicily while the rest of the *Geschwader* took part in the opening stages of Operation *Barbarossa.*

I. *Gruppe* had been in North Africa at the beginning of April and in July, II. *Gruppe* was also re-equipped for the desert war, III. *Gruppe* and the *Geschwaderstab* joined them in Africa in December, where they remained until the Axis powers were forced by the Allied advances to evacuate from Tunisia. The *Stab* moved back to Vienna and then to Athens. I. *Gruppe* was posted to the Channel Coast, II. *Gruppe* remaining in Sicily, withdrawing to the Italian mainland when the island fell. Meanwhile, III *Gruppe* operated over the Aegean islands, based on Rhodes. Here a new IV. *Gruppe* was established and the two *Gruppen* stayed in this area until March 1944.

In July 1943, I. *Gruppe* moved from France to Vienna. II. *Gruppe* joined the other home defence units, but the remainder of the *Geschwader* moved up to fight over the Normandy beachhead and withdrew into Germany as the front moved eastward.

On 1st January 1945, JG 27 joined with IV./JG 54 in the attack on Melsbroek airfield near Brussels, losing 17 pilots, but achieving considerable success. The JG 27 pilots were flying Bf109G-10s, G-14s and K-4s, while the JG 54 element used Fw 190A-8s. During the final withdrawal to Germany, the *Geschwader* was split up. The *Stab* and II. *Gruppe*, retreated to the north, with the remainder going to Prague and later to Salzburg before being disbanded.

This Bf 109E, very obviously in a grey camouflage scheme with white tail band and rudder, carried *Geschwaderadjudant* markings on its yellow cowling and the badge of III. *Gruppe* forward of the cockpit. The two Bf 109s in the background carried spotted desert camouflage, probably applied in the field with available Italian colors.

Above and below left: *Major* Wolfgang Schellmann, somewhere in southeast Europe, with *Ritterkreuz* he received for ten victories during September 1940. Below right: Schellmann and *Generalfeldmarschall* von Richthofen, on a communications radio truck, in Greece.

Left: A young *Leutnant* is inspecting the *Ritterkreuz* of *Oberleutnant* Gustav Rödel.

Above: *Oberleutnant* Gustav Rödel, in the background a camouflaged Bf 109.

Middle left: Rödel (left) and Schroer and comrades.

Bottom left: *Oblt* Gustav Rödel, *Staffelkapitän* of 4./JG 27, visiting what appears to have been a command post of JG 77, another unit which operated in south-eastern Europe.

Gustav Rödel's (Kommodore of JG 27) Bf 109G left back in Sicily.

Knight's Cross holder *Hauptmann* Ernst Börngen of JG 27 who was credited with forty-five victories, and an additional twenty-four that were unconfirmed.

Above and right: Two shots of Karl Schmitz with his Bf 109G-6, "Yellow 4", of 6./JG 27. On the starboard side was the *Staffel* badge and on the port side the *Gruppe* emblem. Aft of the III. *Gruppe* bar was a white fuselage band.

Lt Erbo von Kageneck with his Bf 109E, "Yellow 5", in the spring of 1941 when his rudder indicated fourteen aerial victories. His aircraft carried the grey European theatre color scheme.

Hauptmann Graf Erbo von Kageneck (right), *Staffelkapitän* of 9.III./JG 27 in Bari, Italy. On the left, *Major* Georg Langhoff. Autumn 1941.

Grave of Graf Erbo von Kageneck. As *Staffelkapitän* of 9./JG 27, he was shot down at Christmas 1941 by British fighters and died on January 12, 1942 in a hospital in Neapel. He was one of the top aces at the beginning of the Russian campaign and had a total of sixty-seven victories.

Erbo von Kageneck climbing down from Bf 109 E "Yellow 1" with insignia of III./JG 27. This photograph was taken during August 1941 in Stoltzy on the eastern front.

Feldwebel Heinrich Bartels of 4./JG 27 is showing his 70th victory bar on the white rudder of his Bf 109G-6, "Red 13", W Nr 27 169, at Kalamaki airfield in Greece on November 17, 1943. Rudder also shows his *Ritterkreuz* which he received in the far north at 8./JG 5 for forty-six victories. His last victory (his 99th) was made against a P-47 Thunderbolt, on December 23, 1944 over Bonn. A short time later he was killed in action. His body was found on January 26, 1968 near Villip (Bad Godesberg).

"Yellow 1" and "Yellow 5" of 6./JG 27.

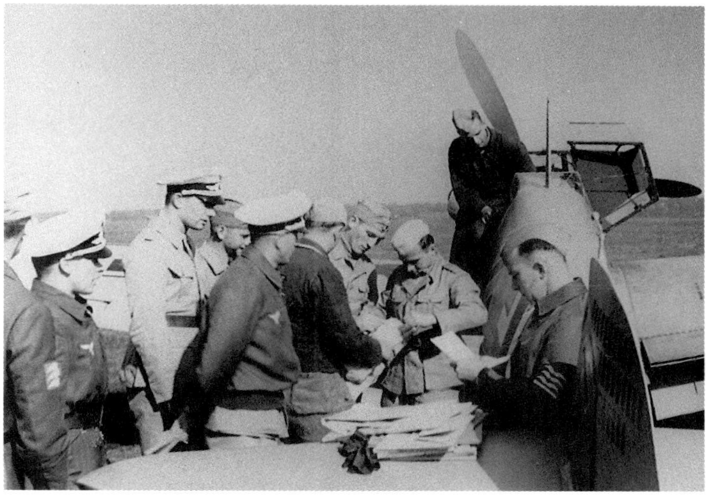

In these two photographs Wolfgang Lippert is seen by the tail of his Bf 109F, W Nr 8469. A fairly new and very clean aircraft, it was camouflaged in 79/78 desert colors, and in addition to the *Gruppenkommandeur* markings on the fuselage, its rudder carried twenty-five victory bars. (Total was 30 victories).

Left: The center of these three Bf 109s was the mount of *Hpt* Wolfgang Lippert of II./JG 27, which displayed the II. *Gruppe* badge on its yellow cowling. Its W Nr was 4148 and there were twenty-one victories shown on its vertical fin. In the foreground was W Nr 4180 showing fifteen victories, the first of which was a Polish aircraft. This was probably Gustav Rödel's aircraft. Right: A close-up of Lippert's tail, with "White 1" of 4. *Staffel* in the background.

Above: An informal shot of a then undistinguished JG 27 pilot, Hans-Joachim Marseille, with a Bf 109E in the background.

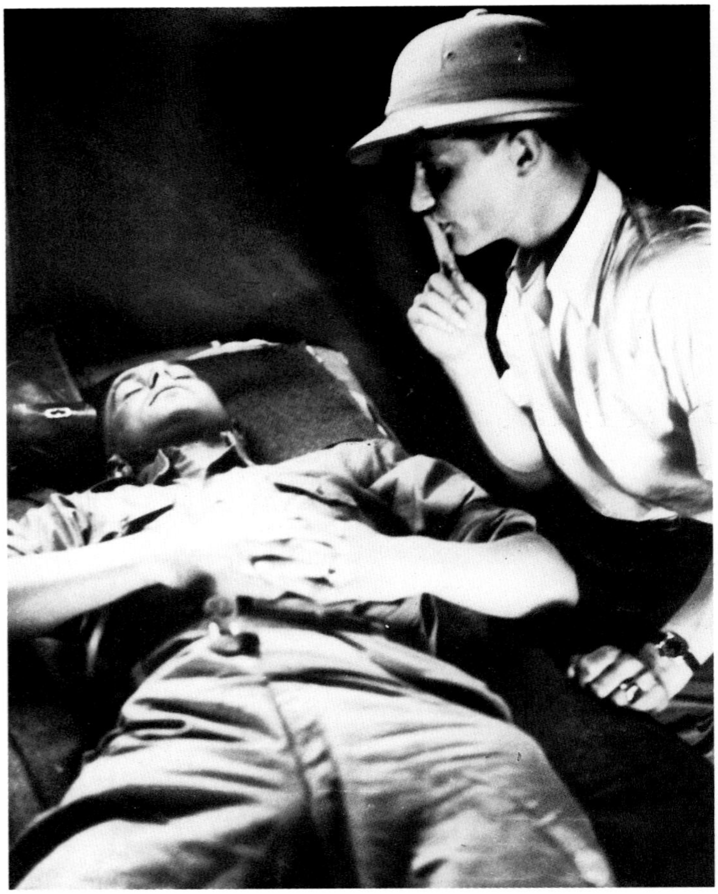

Above right: Lullaby and goodnight . . . Marseille the practical joker.

Right: The rudder of one of the Bf 109Fs, W Nr 8673, flown by Marseille. At the time he was *Staffelkapitän* of 3./JG 27 and had 136 victories as shown on his much-photographed "Yellow 14."

Oblt Rolf Strössner(left), *Staffelkapitän* 6/JG27 from April 1941-January 1942. Just behind can be seen "Yellow 3," "Yellow 6" and "Yellow 2" of 6. *Staffel*. Note the He 111 transport.

"White 13," also a Bf 109F, of 4./JG 27.

Bf 109F, "White 11."

Six Bf 109Fs of 4./JG 27. Note "White 7", "White 10" and "White 5."

A passenger had his parachute harness adjusted before embarking on a flight in this Caudron C455 used by I./JG 27 as a communications aircraft.

Werner Schroer with mechanic and his Bf 109F "< A" in tropical camouflage.

Werner Schroer climbing out of his Bf 109G-5.

Oblt Werner Schroer photographed at an airfield in Sicily with an Italian transport and Bf 109 "Yellow 5" starting up. Such hard surfaces were usually very dusty and contributed to short engine life.

This shot was taken in March 1944 at Wiesbaden-Erbenheim. On the left was Ernst Düllberg, the *Kommandeur* of III./JG 27. Center left was Werner Schroer and in the center, the *Gruppenkommandeur* of II/JG 27 *Hptm* Keller. Düllberg's Bf 109G showed twenty-seven victory markings on the rudder.

Together with his comrades, *Hauptmann* Werner Schroer received the *"Eichenlaub zum Ritterkreuz"* on August 2, 1943 for eighty-four victories. From left: *Hpt* Werner Schroer, *Hpt* Heinrich Ehrler, *Hpt* Egmont Prinz zur Lippe-Weissenfeld, *Major* Helmut Lent, who received the *"Schwerter"*, *Hpt* Manfred Meurer, *Oblt* Joachim Kirschner and *Oblt* Theodor Weissenberger.

Me 262, "White 5", W Nr 111745 of the JV 44 located at München-Riem airfield.

Seated on the long nose of this Fw 190D-9 were, from left, Sachenberg, Wübke, Faber and an unidentified pilot.

Chapter 11

JAGDVERBAND 44

Led from its formation by the legendary Adolf Galland, who had been relieved of his post as *General der Jagdflieger,* unfounded rumors surround this unit like no other in the *Luftwaffe.* JV 44 was established during February 1945 at Brandenburg-Briest with 20 Me 262s. On the same airfield were also the Staff and one *Gruppe* of JG 7 under *Maj* Weissenberger.

After working up on their new jet fighters, JV 44 moved to München-Riem (Munich) in early April with 12 aircraft, and here they were fitted with batteries of R4M rocket projectiles. The unit continued to operate until the last days of the war, but with limited success. They suffered serious losses such as the accident to Johannes Steinhoff on 18th April and the death of Günther Lützow on 24th, whose body still lies in his wreck near Donauwörth where he crashed, looking for the American forces crossing the Donau (Danube). Despite its complement of highly qualified and experienced pilots, the unit's record of successes (only about 50) compares poorly with the similarly equipped JG 7 who counted nearly 500 victories, though this was over a rather longer period and with more aircraft.

From 26th April when he was wounded, Galland handed over command to Heinz Bär, but the end came on 3rd May 1945 when the remaining Me 262s were destroyed on Salzburg airfield in the face of the advancing American army. In the late stages of the war these aircraft had no standard camouflage scheme and no unit emblems; indeed, some had no camouflage at all.

Seen from the left in this photograph: Unknown, Faber, Sachsenberg, and Wübke. They were based at München-Riem airfield on 25th April 1945. In the background was an interesting black and white striped Fw 190 D-9, a type which flew on airfield defence duties for Me 262s as they took off and landed, for it was then that the jets were most vulnerable to attacks by prowling Allied fighters.

Heinz Sachsenberg with his Fw 190 D-9. He accomplished 104 victories.

***Obst* Johannes Steinhoff on an earlier occasion, probably as *Kommodore* of JG 77 in Italy. Just visible is the *Eichenlaub,* which the holders named *Blumenkohl* (cauliflower).**

Chapter 12

JAGDGESCHWADER 51 "MÖLDERS"

The composition of JG 51 was a complicated matter, involving the absorption of several smaller formations into a unit that became an entire Ge*schwader*. I./JG 51 had existed since 1937. In November 1939, a *Geschwaderstab* was established to administer II and III. *Gruppen* also II./JG 51 was formed from I./JG 71 and III.JG 51 had formerly been I./JG 20. During the summer of 1940 a fourth *Gruppe* was added when I/JG 77 became IV./JG 51.

The *Geschwader* was based in the West throughout the early months of war, taking part in the French campaign in May and June 1940 and operating from the Calais area during the Battle of Britain. After re-equipping in Germany during the winter, the unit returned to its French airfields until June 1941 when it was transferred to Poland to support the invasion of Russia. IV. *Gruppe* was attached to JG 53 and operated over the southern sector of the Eastern Front, while the rest of JG 51 was based in the central sector around Bobruisk, Bryansk, Smolensk and Moscow. In August, IV. *Gruppe* rejoined its parent unit. On 24th November 1941, after the death of its former *Kommodore,* Werner Mölders, the unit adopted his name as a title of honor.

During the winter, I. Gr*uppe* was moved to the northern sector and was withdrawn to Jesau during July and August 1942 to be converted from Bf 109s to Fw 190s. Meanwhile, II. *Gruppe* remained in the Orel-Bryansk area.

In June 1942, 15./JG 51 joined II. *Gruppe,* which was composed of Spanish pilots. In October, this *Gruppe* also converted to Fw 190s and was transferred to the Mediterranean theatre, operating successively over Tunisia, Sicily, Italy, Yugoslavia and Hungary, finally ending the war in Vienna.

During the summer of 1944, three *Staffeln* had been withdrawn from Russia to join the units defending Germany itself. The rest of the *Geschwader* retreated to East Prussia in the face of the Soviet advance. In April 1945, I. *Gruppe* was disbanded and many of its personnel became prisoners of the Russians together with some of III. *Gruppe.* The Staff and IV. *Gruppe,* however, withdrew to Schleswig-Holstein and surrendered to British forces. During the entire war JG 51 claimed about 9,000 victories.

Bf 109F-1, WNr 5628, *Stammkennzeichen* " SG + GW" of *Major* Werner Mölders. The rudder shows fifty-four victories, which he had reached by the end of October 1040. Note that the *Stammkennzeichen* was overpainted as well as the engine hood and lower part of rudder. It showed no *Kommodore* markings, or other individual markings.

Werner Mölders, for whom the unit was named after, and his Bf 109 F.

A shot of Mölders Bf 109F-0 " SG + GW" showing fifty-four victories.

Right: A close-up shot of the rudder showing fifty-four victories.

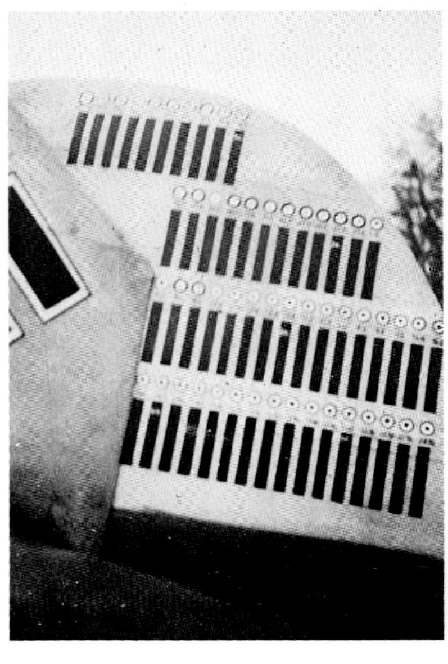

Obstlt **Werner Mölders,** ***Kommodore*** **of JG 51, wearing the** ***Ritterkreuz mit Eichenlaub,*** **awarded on September 21, 1940 for his forty victories.**

Werner Mölders as ***Kommodore*** **of JG 51.**

Werner Mölders with ***Eichenlaub.***

These two photographs show the Bf 109F of Mölders in a camouflaged dispersal pen. The yellow rudder showed fifty-six victories, each marked with an appropriate roundel in four rows, 10, 12, 16 and 18.

Above: This shot is especially interesting because it is one of the few photographs to show an entire view of any of Werner Mölders' aircraft. It is reputed to have been taken at Wiesbaden in June 1941. At this time there were five rows of victory markings on the rudder, a total of sixty-five, and a large *Geschwader* falcon emblem on its yellow cowling. Perhaps oddly for an F model, it carried a 71/02/65 camouflage scheme.

Left: On the rudder of this aircraft, almost certainly an earlier on used by Mölders, were fifty-five bars on a background of what appears to be pale blue-grey 65.

Mölders in front of his aircraft. Note the falcon emblem of JG 51.

Mölders in the cockpit of a Bf 109.

Two aircraft of 7./JG 51, "White 7" and "White 8."

Three Bf 109Es of 7./JG 51 in the dark green 70/71 camouflage in use during 1939. Shown here were "White 4", "White 1" and "White 9."

Bf 109E, "White 9" of 7./JG 51. On engine hood is "bow and arrow" emblem of 7th *staffel*, formerly used by 1./JG 20. In the background "White 11", in the sky are two other aircraft, forming the smallest unit, a "Rotte." All aircraft in early standard camouflage, 70/71 and 65.

Mechanics of 6./JG 51 "making music." Note oil container and Bf 109Es in the background.

"Yellow 8", a very new Bf 109E of 6./JG 51 at Böblingen in April 1940. Behind is "Yellow 1."

The fuselage sides of these two Bf 109Es seen at Böblingen in April 1940 were more densely camouflaged than usual. The II/JG 51 emblem, consisting of a raven with an umbrella under its wing, can be seen aft of the fuselage cross on the second aircraft.

Bf 109 E "Red 5 or 7" showing black cat emblem of 8./JG 51.

Mechanics working on Bf 109E of 8./JG 51.

Two photos above and two opposite: Mechanics rearming Bf 109E, "Red 10" of 8./JG 51 *Staffel*, also with the black cat symbol on engine hood; on MG 17 ammunition box is W Nr of aircraft, 3396. Also note space behind engine hood where ammunition boxes were stored.

Bf 109 of famous Josef Priller, here in the markings of a *Staffelkapitän* of 6./JG 51. Note: rudder in light yellow, twenty white victory bars on the fin, II./JG 51 emblem behind the *Balkenkreuz* ("Gott strafe England"), "Yellow 1" and "heart-ace" card, personal emblem of Priller. Engine-hood was dark yellow and total aircraft was heavily camouflaged with RLM 71. On October 19, 1940, Priller received the *Ritterkreuz* as *Oberleutnant* for twenty victories.

Priller climbing in a "normal" camouflaged Bf 109E.

Eutingen airfield during December 1939. From left, Priller, *Oberfeldwebel* Gläser and *Hfw* Herpfer. In the background a Bf 109E with unusual dark camouflaged upper-part of the rudder.

Oberleutnant Priller in his car.

A musical interlude with Josef Priller and Sepp Wiedmann. Behind them was *Oblt* Werner Knittel, *Adjudant* of II. *Gruppe,* who was lost over England on October 28, 1940. In 1973 his remains were found at Burmarsh, Kent, in the wreckage of his Bf 109E, W Nr 5095, and were given proper burial.

Crashed aircraft of *Uffz* Seidel, a Bf 109E in Bölingen on May15, 1940.

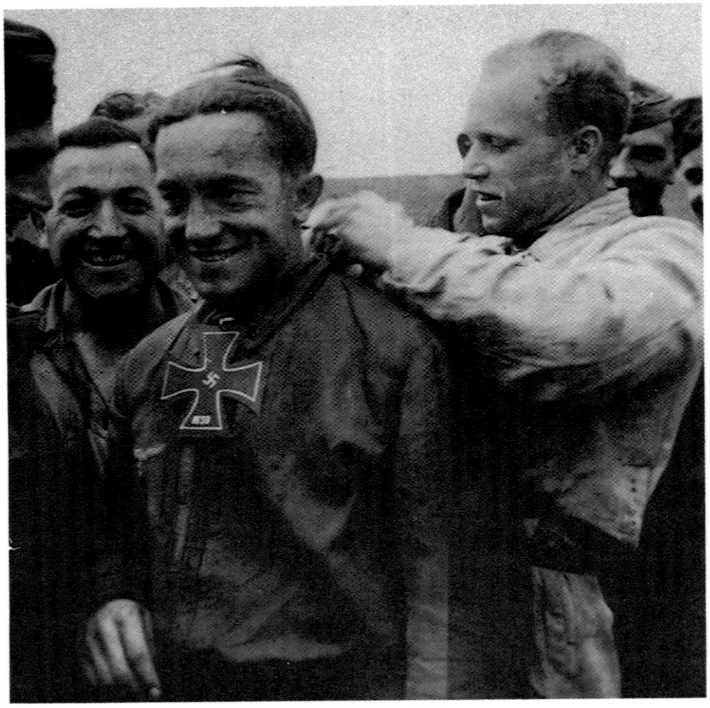

Top scoring JG 51 pilot with a total of 204 victories, Anton Hafner, is shown receiving an enlarged copy of the *Ritterkreuz* that he received on August 23, 1942 for sixty victories as *Feldwebel.*

This II./JG 51 aircraft photographed in March 1940 was completely devoid of individual markings. The upper surfaces were the then standard colors of dark green 71 and grey 02.

This Fw 190, "Yellow 1", force-landed near Orel, Russia, in June 1943. The pilot, Herbert Bareuther, was the *Staffelkapitän* of 3./JG 51 and after recording fifty-five victories, was shot down in 14./JG 3 on April 30, 1945. He is believed to have been awarded the *Ritterkreuz* during the last days of the war.

Several Fw 190s of 3./JG 51. The second machine from the left was Bareuther's "Yellow 1", although the color of the code has also been described as brown.

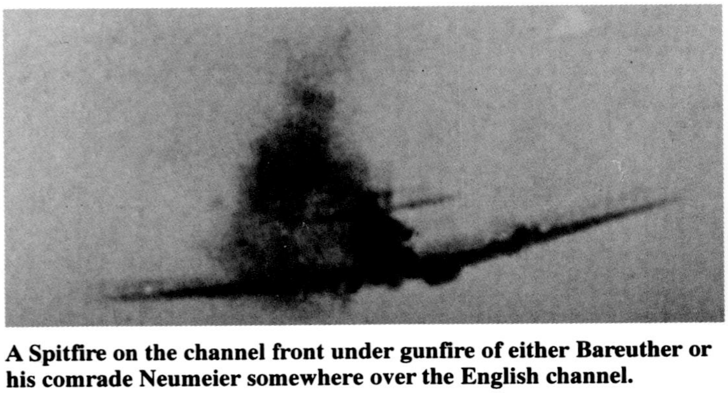

A Spitfire on the channel front under gunfire of either Bareuther or his comrade Neumeier somewhere over the English channel.

Above and below: Another victim of poor pilot visibility during taxiing was the Fw 190, "Yellow 3", W Nr 0636, which crashed with a Fw 190A-8, during an alarm take off at Terespol, PL. Note late form of swastika.

Above and below left: Helmut Johne of the Stabstaffel/JG 51, photographed in November 1944. His Fw 190A-8 carried black *Stab* markings and the number 3 on a rather patchy grey camouflage scheme. The spinner and nose rings were yellow. Below right: A camouflaged Fw 190 between houses in Memel Airfield, 1944.

Lothar Busse climbing out of his Bf 109G-6 in Ezere, Kurland during September 1944.

Camouflaged Bf 109 of Lothar Busse near Warzawa, also during September 1944.

Uffz Bach, also of Stabstaffel/JG 51, in his aircraft "15." His Fw 190A-8, W Nr 7322...?, had the same camouflage as that of Johne's aircraft.

Uffz **Merbeler with mechanic Franz Breitler in his aircraft "12" of Stabstaffel/JG 51 W Nr 732090. Please note, no fuselage band on all aircraft. Merbeler had a total of twelve victories and died during air-battle on March 26, 1945.**

Above: Oblt Martin with a Bf 109G at Schalatowka in 1944. The aircraft carried white winter camouflage with a yellow tail band and rudder.

Above and two photos below: The crashed Bf 109G "Yellow 15" of *Oblt* Werner Martin. During an alarm take off he came into the slip-stream of another aircraft causing a fatal crash. *Oblt* Martin was a long-time *Rottenflieger* of Dr. Lange, who later became *Kommodore*. But at this time, during 1944 in Ostpreussen, he was not in this Gruppe. Note very light colored aircraft sides, dead pilot is still lying nearby.

Very light camouflaged Bf 109G-5 crashed in East Prussia 1944. "Yellow 4" marking is nearly invisible, spinner was light yellow with red spiral. Aircraft belonged to Walter Wever, Staffelkapitän of 3./JG 51. He received the *Ritterkreuz* for forty-four victories during January 1945 and had a fatal crash with a Me 262, as a member of JG 7, during April 1945.

Oberfeldwebel Alfred Rauch received the *Ritterkreuz* for fifty-three victories during April 1945, and had a total of sixty.

Unteroffizier Franz Josef Beerenbrock with *Ritterkreuz*. Later he received the *Eichenlaub* and had a total of 117 victories when he was shot down near Welish, SU on November 9, 1942. One of the few highly decorated pilots who survived early imprisonment in Russia.

Left: Herrman Friedrich Joppien, *Kommandeur* of I./JG 51. For twenty-one victories in the west he received the *Ritterkreuz*, for forty victories the *Eichenlaub*. After reaching seventy victories in the east he had a fatal crash near Brijansk, SU during August 1941.

Below: Bf 109G on weapon adjustment stand in Terespol, PL. Note 3 circles on target for the two MG 131 and engine mounted cannon.

The four photos above show an Fw 190 under repair in Smolensk during September 1943. Note details of aircraft, and oversprayed propeller blades in yellow.

Above: This bruised and upended Fw 190, "Brown 2" of 2. *Staffel,* appears to have included some especially dark areas in its camouflage, which was otherwise the usual 74/75/76, albeit somewhat deteriorated due to operational use. Top right: Fw 190 "Yellow 2" of 3./JG 51. Aircraft had a non-standard camouflage, including green colors. Below: Parked Fw 190 at Sytschewka, SU during August 1943. Note also yellow propeller blades in the same color as spinner.

Armament mechanic Gaibler posing as a pilot in front of a Fw 190.

Bf 109G in white winter camouflage and mechanic Gaibler, probably in Schalatowka, Autumn 1942.

Above: Feldwebel Schweigert (left) and Kirchenbauer in front of "Yellow 1" of Bareuther. Both aircraft had a very dark camouflage.

"Yellow 8" of 3./JG 51 in a tiger-stripe style of camouflage which presents something of a problem to identify positively.

Right: Fw 190 of Stab/JG 51 taking off at Modlin PL when unit was trained for Fw 190.

"Ben" Benedikt Haupt sitting in a Bf 109G.

"Ben" Benedikt Haupt, Orscha 1943, showing the EK I.

Above: Pilots of I./JG 51. In the front left, Bareuther and "Ben" Haupt. Standing at the right, Erich Neuner.

Left: "Yellow 2" of "Ben" Haupt in Orel 1943. On the right, Helmut Behrendt; by the wing, Hans Peetz.

Bf 109G "Black 11" in winter camouflage and Paul Messmer in the cockpit. He had a fatal crash on January 16, 1945 at Ziechenau (Poland) airfield.

Fw 190 "Yellow 4" with yellow fuselage band. From left, *Feldwebel* Häse (?), *Uffz* Haase and in the right foreground is *Staffelkapitän* of 3./JG 51, *Hauptmann* Heinz Lange, who later became *Kommodore.* He had a total of seventy victories and received the *Ritterkreuz* during November 1944.

Here, Paul Messmer was being carried by fellow airmen after another victory. On his Fw 190 in the background the winter camouflage had almost worn through to the paintwork underneath.

Oberleutnant Niemaier climbing out of his Fw 190. Nickname of Niemaier was "Bepl."

Ltn Sturm, leader of the so-called "Sturm-staffel," the Stabsstaffel.

Stabsstaffel during August 1944, right beside Sturm is *Leutnant* Wilhelm Hübner a *Ritterkreuzträger* with sixty-two victories. He died during April 1945 near Neukuhren/Ostpreussen. Nearly all of his pilots were lost in the war.

Above: Unknown pilots of JG 51.

Center right and right: Bf 109F belonging to *Leutnant* Hans Strelow, of 5/JG 51. At the end of January 1942 he led this Staffel as a teenager. On March 18, 1942, just eight days before his 20th birthday, he achieved seven victories making his total at this time fifty-nine. For this he received the *Ritterkreuz* and just six days after received the *Eichenlaub* for his sixty-sixth victory. After a holiday at home, he returned to the front at the beginning of May 1942. His tragical end came on May 22, 1942 when he shot down his sixty-eighth and last victim, a Pe-2 aircraft. Already falling down in his aircraft, the tail gunner shot down Strelow in his Bf 109 F "Black 10" and he had to bail out east of Mszensk, 9km behind the front line. Surrounded by Russian soldiers, he shot himself.

Armor-mechanic Gaibler with a winter-camouflaged Bf 109G on which even the propeller blades had been overpainted.

Gaibler and Behrend, two mechanics in Brijansk 1943, SU.

Above: Gaibler in front of a Fw 190.

Right: Fw 190 with MGFF; Gaibler is in the cockpit.

Bf 109 "Yellow 12" with mechanics of JG 51.

Mechanics of JG 51 in front of a Bf 109F.

Bf 109G in Schalatowka 1944, with mechanics.

MG 151/20 of a Fw 190 under inspection. Note dark camouflage of aircraft.

One of JG 51's Bf 109Fs in a revetment at Syelce, Poland, in June 1941. Clearly visible are the three hinged cowling sections with the removable section ahead of the windscreen on the ground under the starboard wing.

From about 1943 onward, as new types of high performance Russian fighters were produced, *Luftwaffe* pilots found it increasingly difficult to maintain their aerial supremacy. "Brown 7", a Fw 190 of JG 51, had obviously seen hard operational use on the Eastern Front.

Left: A pair of Bf 109Gs preparing to take off in front of a Ju 188 whose last two code letters were LM. It is believed the numerals of these two Messerchmitts were painted brown rather than the more usual yellow.

Bf 109F, "Yellow 7", of the JG 51, showing forty-three victories on the rudder.

Bf 109G of III./JG 51, somewhere in Italy. Note white (Mediterranean) fuselage band.

Above: Bf 109Es of JG 51. Below: Crews form earthen revetments for JG 51 fighters.

Günther Rall, with a total of 275 victories, is seen here with his *Ritterkreuz mit Eichenlaub und Schwertern*.

Chapter 13

JAGDGESCHWADER 52

It was not until the spring of 1940 that third *Gruppe* of JG 52 was established to join I. and II. *Gruppen* which had been defending the Franco-German frontier since the outbreak of war. The entire *Geschwader* fought in the French campaign and occupied bases on the Channel Coast to take part in the Battle of Britain, although III. *Gruppe* withdrew to Germany before going to Romania in October. I./JG 52 remained in France and the Netherlands until September 1941, the II. *Gruppe* and Staff only till May 1941, when they moved east in preparation for *Barbarossa*. Meanwhile, III. *Gruppe* had taken part in the Cretan operation during May, withdrawing again to Romania before moving up to the southern sector of the Eastern Front. While in the east, the *Geschwader* was joined by a 15. (Croat) *Staffel* and a 13. (Slovak) *Staffel* which operated until the end of 1943.

Early in 1942, the I. and II. *Gruppen* were re-equipped in Germany, returning to take part in the big summer offensive in which they gained many victories in the central and southern sectors. When the Crimea was lost, however, the *Geschwader* was split up, with three *Staffeln* (one from each *Gruppe*) being allocated during May 1944 to home defence duties. II. *Gruppe* retreated through Romania and Hungary to Vienna and surrendered at the end of hostilities at Graz and Bad Aibling. The Staff, with the other two *Gruppen,* moved back first to Romania, but then to Poland, the Kurland pocket, East Prussia and Silesia, finally surrendering to the American 90th Division at Böhmen. The Americans handed over their prisoners to the Russians. For many JG 52 personnel, such as Erich Hartmann, this meant ten years of captivity in the Soviet Union.

During the entire period of its existence, JG 52 was equipped with successive models of the Bf 109, reputedly gaining about 11,000 victories, thus making it the most successful *Luftwaffe* fighter unit of the war.

Günther Rall and Bf 109G-3.

The three Graf brothers. From the left: Wilhelm, Hermann, and Josef, sitting on a Bf 109G-6 of *Stab.*/JG 52.

Left: Hermann Graf leaving a Ju 52 in Konstanz, during a visit from the front, showing *Ritterkreuz mit Eichenlaub* und *Schwerter*, which he received for 105 victories during May 1942.

Above: Hermann Graf climbing from a yellow-nosed Bf 109E, "Yellow 4," at a training unit.

Above: *Major* Hermann Graf showing the *"Ritterkreuz mit Eichenlaub, Schwerter* und *Brillianten,"* which he received on September 16, 1942 when he reached 172 victories, clearly surpassing Gordon Gollob, the top scorer until now.

Above: Major Hermann Graf.

Left: Hermann Graf in front of the restaurant "Linde" in Engen surrounded by comrades of the famous Luftwaffe "red hunter" soccer team. To his right is Fritz Walter, a member of the post-war world champion team.

Wilhelm Graf leaving a Bf 109G-6 of the *Geschwaderstab* on which the bar had been overpainted with a whitewash.

Wilhelm Graf in the cockpit of his Bf 109G-6.

Wilhelm Graf sitting with mechanic on the wing of his Bf 109G-6, also in white winter camouflage.

Wilhelm Graf with his Bf 109G. In the background a Bf 109G and a Fw 190. The Fw 190 was never used by JG 52.

Wilhelm Graf in the cockpit of his Bf 109G-6.

Above: *Major* Johannes Wiese with *Eichenlaub* which he received on March 2, 1944 for 125 victories. He had a total of 133 confirmed and further seventy-five unconfirmed victories.

Below: *Hpt* Wiese with is Bf 109G-2/R6, "Black", which was painted in unusually dark and solid camouflage, probably grey 74.

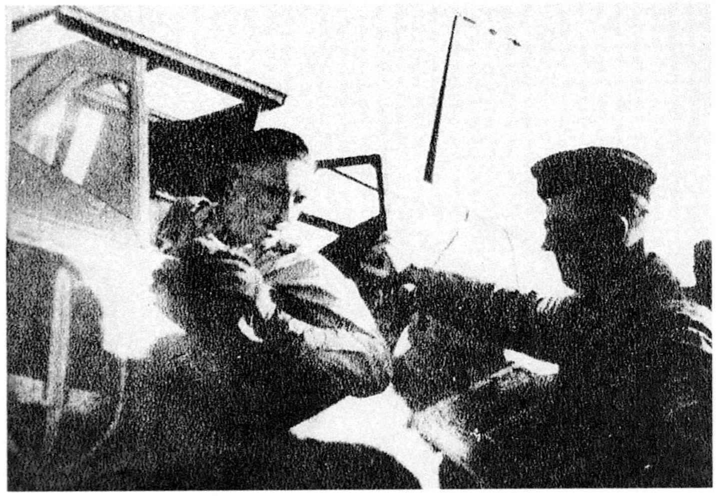

Above: Wiese's Bf 109G as *Gruppenkommandeur* with JG 52 emblem.

Below: *Major* Johannes Wiese with *Eichenlaub*.

Above: Johannes Wiese of JG 52 photographed in July 1943 after his 100th victory. He was later credited with a further thirty-three confirmed.

Above: Johannes Wiese of "White 1", a Bf 109G-2 of I./JG 52, is celebrating his sixtieth victory at Orel.

Below: *Hauptmann* Wiese with his comrades *Oberfeldwebel* Trenkel and *Oberleutnant* Dähne.

Below: *Hauptmann* Johannes Wiese with *Ritterkreuz.*

Above: This photograph taken on March 2, 1944 shows a group of airmen parading before Adolf Hitler for the award of the *Eichenlaub*. From the left were *Maj* Bühligen of JG 2, *Hpt* Wiese of JG 52, unknown (but not a fighter pilot), *Maj* Seiler of JG 104, *Hpt* Ademeit of JG 54, *Oblt* Krupinski of JG 52 and *Lt* Hartmann, also of JG 52.

Left: The face of Johannes Wiese is showing the wear of the just finished air battle.

Below: The aircraft in 74/75 and 76 camouflage just stopped.

The interesting series of shots here and on the following two pages show Johannes Wiese and Bf 109G-6 coming back to the airfield when he had just made his 100th victory during July 1943. His machine had rather faded standard 74/75/76 camouflage, including the rudder, which carried no victory bars at this time. Note low contrast upperside camouflage, yellow tail band, fuselage Balkenkreuz in 74, wheel bumps, thin upper wing Balkenkreuz in white, black swastika and dark spots on rudder. Comrades had made a wreath with shield showing: "Wir gratulieren zum 100. Luftsieg." "We congratulate you on your 100th victory." Holding the Perspex model of Icarus is Karl-Heinz Plücker, who had a total of forty-two victories (2.Staffel).

WL
410153

100.

100.

These three photos show the Bf 109E of *Hauptmann* Herbert Ihlefeld, *Gruppenkommandeur*. Taken around July 1941, in Jassy, Romania. Rudder is showing a total of forty-six victories, thirty-six in the west and ten in the east. At this time he had already been decorated with the *Eichenlaub* (Oak leaves), for forty victories on June 27, 1941. He had achieved a total of 132 victories, including fifteen four-engined bombers and flew on over 1000 missions.

Above and below: ***Major*** **Ihlefeld,** ***Kommodore*** **of JG 52 in front of a W 34 surrounded by JG 52 personnel.**

Above, right, and below: ***Leutnant*** **Walter Krupinski in his Bf 109G-1 "Yellow 5" of II./JG 52. Photos were taken at the time when he received the** ***Ritterkreuz*** **during October 1942 for fifty-three victories. He had a total of 197 victories.**

Bf 109G-2 of the *Gruppenkommandeur* of I./JG 52, Helmut Bennemann. As a memory to his time on the channel front he used the old I./JG 52 emblem, the black hand, grabbing after the Spitfire.

Two photos above: This Bf 109G-2 was flown by Helmut Bennemann, *Kommandeur* of I. *Gruppe*. To recall the period in which he served on the Channel Coast, he had retained the former *Gruppe* emblem of a black and white hand clawing at a Spitfire. The flying kit hanging on the pitot tube is of interest.

Above: Bennemann about to celebrate a notable victory. The aircraft, probably an earlier *Gustav*, carried the markings of an *Adjudant*. Right: Note dark camouflage color of aircraft.

Hpt **Helmut Bennemann, the pilot of this JG 52 Bf 109F, seen putting into practice his own ideas on camouflage. One can only speculate about the colors.**

Bennemann climbing out of his Bf 109E at the channel front.

Oblt **Bennemann inspecting bullet holes in his Bf 109E after returning from a mission. The badge was that of I.** ***Gruppe.***

Above: *Hpt* Bennemann's same Bf 109G-2, now in winter camouflage. Note the heavy smoke stains around the exhaust and gun ports.

Right: Another shot of the machine above, with Bennemann and one of his mechanics.

Above: *Oberleutnant* Bennemann making music at Esbjerg, DK during 1941. Note unusual three color spinner of Bf 109F in the background.

Center right: *Hauptmann* Sepi, in the background *Oberleutnant* Bennemann.

Right: Three *Ritterkreuz* holders celebrating JG 52's 5,000th victory at Taman in Russia. From left: *Maj* Hrabak, *Hpt* Bennemann, *Hpt* Rall.

Above: Walking away from his Bf 109F was *Maj* Trübenbach, JG 52's *Kommodore* in 1941.

Right: Trübenbach's aircraft raises a cloud of dust as it taxies out for take-off. Noteworthy features are the yellow cowling, fuselage band and *Kommodore* marking.

Below: *Major* Trübenbach (left) looking at his Bf 109F, W Nr 7090, when tail wheel collapsed.

When this photograph was taken in July 1941, there were twenty-one victories shown on the tail of Karl Heinz Leesmann's Bf 109F. He was then *Kommandeur* of I. *Gruppe*, whose emblem appeared on the rear fuselage of his aircraft.

***Oberleutnant* Leesmann showing Ritterkreuz.**

Above and below: Leesmann's earlier Bf 109E, W Nr 5065, showing nine and eleven victories respectively during 1940.

Hpt Johannes Steinhoff in the Crimea in 1942 as *Kommandeur* of II./ JG 52 with his Bf 109G-3. He ended the war in the hospital as a result of a serious crash after achieving 176 victories.

Feldwebel Heinz Schmidt of 6./JG 52 in his Bf 109F during the summer of 1941. This aircraft "Black 3" carried a "Eri"!-sign with flowers. ERI was the aircraft of Johannes Wiese "Black 5."

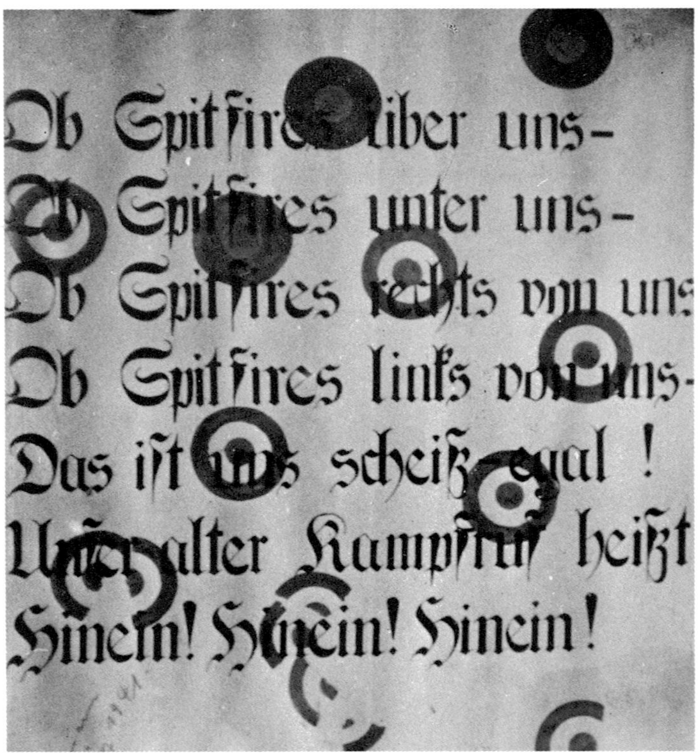

Above: A Bf 109E of 2. *Staffel* over the English Channel. It carried the unit badge of JG 52 under the cockpit and the shield of I. *Gruppe* on its yellow cowling. Right. "Spitfires over us, Spitfires under us . . .", a battle song popular with JG 52.

Right: The I./JG 52 emblem in detail. On the background of blue and white was a black running boar, the lower dark section being red, with a white border thinly outlined in black.

Lt Wolfgang Ewald of 2./JG 52 and his yellow-nosed Bf 109E. Ewald had just returned from a mission over the English Channel in which he claimed another of his eventual total of seventy-eight victories.

Oberleutnant Dähne back from a mission in the east.

Jagdführer Carl Schumacher visiting JG 52 in the west, probably Texel. It seems that he also used Stabs-marking on his Bf 109F.

Above and below: Wiese, Hrabak and Dähne in front of the Bf 109G-6, "Black 4" of *Staffelkapitän* Dähne of 2./JG 52.

Wiese, Hrabak and Dähne, the *Staffelkapitän* , with the latter's Bf 109G-6, "Black 4." The softly sprayed and probably faded camouflage was very light in appearance.

Lt Berthel's appropriately numbered "Red 1" at Bonn-Hangelar during the autumn of 1939. In this machine Berthel claimed I/JG 52s first victory in the war. At this time the second *Staffel* numbers were usually red rather than black.

"Red 1" again, during the very cold winter of 1939-40. Maintaining aircraft under such trying conditions was very demanding on the ground crews.

"Red 1" a Bf 109E, W Nr 3335 at Bonn-Hangelar on October 6, 1939. With this aircraft *Leutnant* Berthel made the first air victory of the I/JG 52, a French Leo 63. The dark 70/71 camouflage and swastika centrally located on the rudder hinge line were standard for the period.

The first victory bar being added to *Lt* Berthel's Bf 109E, W Nr 3335, at Bonn-Hangelar on October 6, 1939.

Congratulations for *Leutnant* Berthel for his victory, the first of the I/JG 52.

Part of the tail of Berthels's unfortunate victim.

Ofw Gerber in the aircraft in which he had just claimed a victory somewhere in the west.

Mechanics are happy about the victory of *Oberfeldwebel* Gerber.

Karl Munz in his Bf 109#, "Black 3". He was awarded the *Ritterkreuz* in the last weeks of the war for his sixtieth victory.

Hpt Helmut Kühle in his "Yellow 1", with *Oblt* Horst Tietzen by the cockpit. Tietzen, already a *Ritterkreuzträger* in 1940, was the fourth pilot to reach twenty victories but was shot down over the Channel on August 18, 1940.

Mechanics sitting on a Bf 109F fitted with additional underwing armament. In the background was an aircraft bearing *Adjutant* markings.

Shown inside this hangar were several Bf 109Fs of JG 52, the one on the right being fitted with underwing gondolas for two 30mm MK 108 cannon.

"Fritz had made a victory," this picture was titled. In the background the aircraft "Black 4" of the unknown Leutnant.

Two more Bf 109Fs of JG 52, the machine on the right being fitted with underwing gondolas. The one on the left was coded "Yellow 2."

Another Bf 109G of JG 52, this one having the black and white spiral spinner marking introduced in July 1944.

Bf 109Es with white wingtips are starting at Calais, France.

Crashed Bf 109E "Yellow 2" of 3./JG 52.

Above and below: Crashed Bf 109E "Yellow 7" of 3rd Staffel near Hoppenstätten.

The Bf 109's narrow-track undercarriage was a shortcoming which continued to plague it for years. Moving an aircraft as deeply bogged as "Yellow 6" was a time consuming and troublesome procedure.

Dietrich Hrabak, *Kommodore* of JG 52, in the cockpit of his Bf 109G with, from left, Friedrich Obleser and Karl Gratz, both of 8./JG 52 and on the right, Erich Hartmann of 9./JG 52.

***Oblt* Wilhelm Batz, *Hpt* Gerhard Barkhorn and *Lt* Heinrich Sturm in front of Batz's Bf 109G of 5./JG 52. The photograph was taken around autumn, 1943.**

Erich Hartmann being welcomed home on August 25, 1944 on the occasion of his 301st victory, eleven of them being claimed that day. On the pole was the *Karaya* emblem of 9./JG 52.

Photographed here on July 25, 1943 after achieving 5./JG 52's 500th victory was Peter Düttman. His aircraft "Black 12", was a Bf 109G-4.

A Bf 109F," Yellow 1", of III./JG 52.

A Bf 109G of JG 52.

Lightly-camouflaged Bf 109Es of JG 52 dispersed around Charleville airfield in France during May 1940.

Practically the whole of I. *Gruppe* appears to be using Charleville airfield in this shot taken during the French campaign in May 1940, with over twenty aircraft being visible.

Uffz Eugen Kind dozing in front of his Bf 109E. in the event of an emergency take-off, the tarpaulins and nets could be speedily removed. Kind was shot down over Kent on September 5, 1940.

A JG 52 *Emil*, partly hidden from the air, being readied for operations. Wherever possible, revetments were built near trees to afford maximum natural protection, a basic dictum of effective camouflage.

This partially dismantled Bf 109E, "Black 15", presented a sad sight before it could be moved elsewhere for repair. It had crash-landed, probably having run out of fuel during combat. Being so exposed, it was a vulnerable target for enemy aircraft, hence the camouflage netting.

An interesting shot of two Bf 109Es of JG 52, "Black 15" and "Black 1", taken somewhere in the West during early 1940. The 71/02/65 camouflage scheme is clearly discernable on the near aircraft.

Bf 109Es at Frankfurt airport during transfer to Magdeburg.

"Black 11" of JG 52 having its guns adjusted about mid-1940. By this time the former hard upper/lower surface camouflage separation line on the fuselage had been softened by an overspray of RLM 02.

Bf 109E, "Black 3" of JG 52, undergoing maintenance in 1940. The forward cowling clearly shows the running boar unit emblem.

"Red 4", a 71/02/65-camouflaged Bf 109E of I./JG 52 undergoing maintenance and armament adjustments during early 1940. The high color separation line helped provide good air-to-air concealment.

Above and below: Soccer team of the unit in front of a Bf 109F. Rudder and engine cowling was yellow.

Partly camouflaged Bf 109Fs of I./JG 52 ready for action at a moment's notice.

Above: Bf 109G "< 5" with mechanics. Below: A Bf 109G-6 needs oil also!

Bf 109, somewhere in the east. The soldiers are waiting for the next transfer. In the background "Black 7", in the foreground left, *Oberfeldwebel* Rudolf Trenkel, a *Ritterkreuzträger* with 138 victories.

Above: A mechanic refilling ammunition for the MG 131 (13mm) of a Bf 109G-6. Below: The mechanic is finished.

An unidentified Bf 109G on the Eastern Front. In late 1940 JG 52 began adding numerals to the *Stab* symbols to a much greater extent than other units, although the practice dated back to pre-war days.

Members of JG 52 appraising a newly-delivered Bf 109G-6 which still carried its radio call-signs.

An unidentified Bf 109G-6 belonging to JG 52 and bearing *Adjutant* markings.

Left and above: Bf 109G-6 with *Adjutant* markings.

Center left, left and above: Bf 109G-6 of the *Kommodore,* probably that of *Major* Hrabak.

Two photos above, above right and right: Bf 109G-6 of the *Gruppenkommandeur* of I./JG 52.

Above: Good luck for "Red 13." The unusually thick style of the numbers is a noteworthy feature.

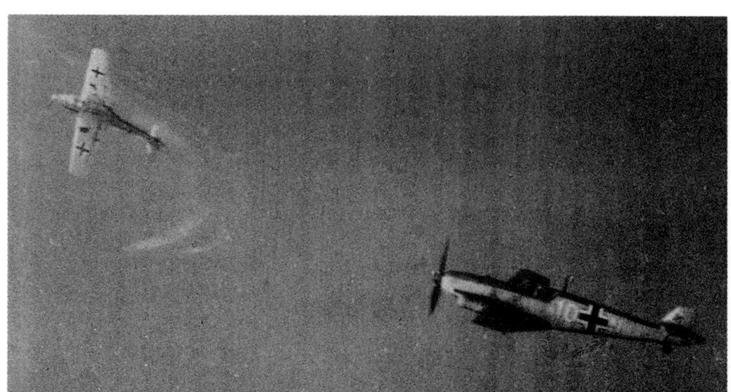

Right: A mock combat between two Bf 109Ds, the pursuing aircraft being coded 10+N.

"White 4" has its oxygen bottles replenished at a forward base. Under the cockpit was JG 52's red, black, silver and white dagger emblem and aft of the fuselage cross, the badge of I. *Gruppe*.

Three Bf 109s at the scenic location of Hoppstädten, all aircraft carrying the 71/02/65 camouflage scheme and the I. *Gruppe* badge on their cowlings.

"White 3" of JG 52 undergoing maintenance in a blast pen during 1939. Behind the fuselage cross was the running boar *Gruppe* insigne. Because of the angle of the strong late afternoon sunlight, the dark camouflage appears much lighter than usual.

Camouflaged Bf 109E at Böhringen-Hardt.

Except for the spotted aircraft on the right, most of these 3./JG 52 Bf 109Es photographed at Laachen-Speyerdorf in October 1939 were finished in the 70/71/65 scheme standard at the time.

Different camouflaged Bf 109E of 3rd Staffel at Laachen-Speyerdorf during October 1939.

"White 5", another casualty, this time of JG 52. The style of fuselage cross makes an interesting comparison.

Above: Crashed Bf 109E of Beutler with Hermann Hoes between the wreck of this EJG 53 aircraft.

Left: Damaged Bf 109F of III Gruppe.

Airfield with Bf 109G somewhere in Russia.

Airfield with Bf 109G, in the foreground "Yellow 8" showing about twenty-seven victories on the rudder.

Heinrich Füllgrabe, an ace of JG 52 with sixty-five victories, here in a Bf 108 "Taifun."

Bf 109E of I./JG 52 under repair.

From left: Sturm, Hrabak and Batz. Besides the ace Wilhelm Batz, with 237 victories, Heinrich Sturm had 157 victories – one of the very successful pilots of the unit.

Personnel of 2./JG 52. From left: *Lt* Schneider, *Ofw* Trenkel, *Lt* Karl Rung, *Ofw* Georg Schwientek, *Lt* P.H. Dähne ("Sarotti"), *Ofw* Grassmuck *Kommodore Hpt* Bennemann, *Uffz* Tölle, *Gen* Fiebig, *Oblt* Miethig, *Hpt* Wiese.

Mechanics of I./JG 52 during their lunch break.

A Bf 109G of the Hungarian *Staffel* with its distinctive red, white, and green tail markings. The pilots were, from the left: *Oblt* Miethig, *Oblt* Banloky Föhodnodj, the *Staffelkapitän*, *Hpt* Bennemann, *Hpt* Josef Haiböck and *Oblt* Geissler.

A lucky charm, in this case a rag doll, was often a companion to pilots on operations. The cockpit is that of a Bf 109E.

The *Staffel* flag here showed the emblem of 3./JG 52. It represented Neville Chamberlain's well-known umbrella being shot to pieces. Chamberlain was Prime Minister of Britain until May 1940.

These two photos of three *Ritterkreuz* holders, were taken in September or October 1942 and in front of Günther Rall's Bf 109G-2, "Black 13." The photo on the left shows from left to right, *Uffz* Karl Gratz, *Oblt* Günther Rall and *Uffz* Friedrich Wachowiak and the photo on the right shows Wachowiak on the left followed by Rall and Gratz.

AIRCRAFT IN DETAIL

Drawings by R. Sandow

In most cases with the black and white drawings which follow, it has proved an impossible task to establish the corresponding upper surface patterns of the specific aircraft concerned. Any photographs or combinations of photographs which show complete top views of *any* fighter aircraft, for that matter, are either extremely rare or simply do not exist. Scarce as this information is, the most comprehensive coverage of the subject is still Kookaburra's four-part reference series on *Luftwaffe* camouflage and markings, to which has now been added a completely new volume covering the 1935–40 period.

Although the aircraft colors described in the following selection represent the most up-to-date conclusions of a team comprising some of the world's most experienced color researchers, it must be appreciated that one-hundred-percent accuracy in identification of all colors in each and every case is a practical impossibility. Strong *probability* of accuracy is the best that can ever be hoped for. Where doubt exists as to the true colors, this is plainly stated on the drawing concerned.

Bf 109E, W Nr 3335, Red 1 of I./JG 52

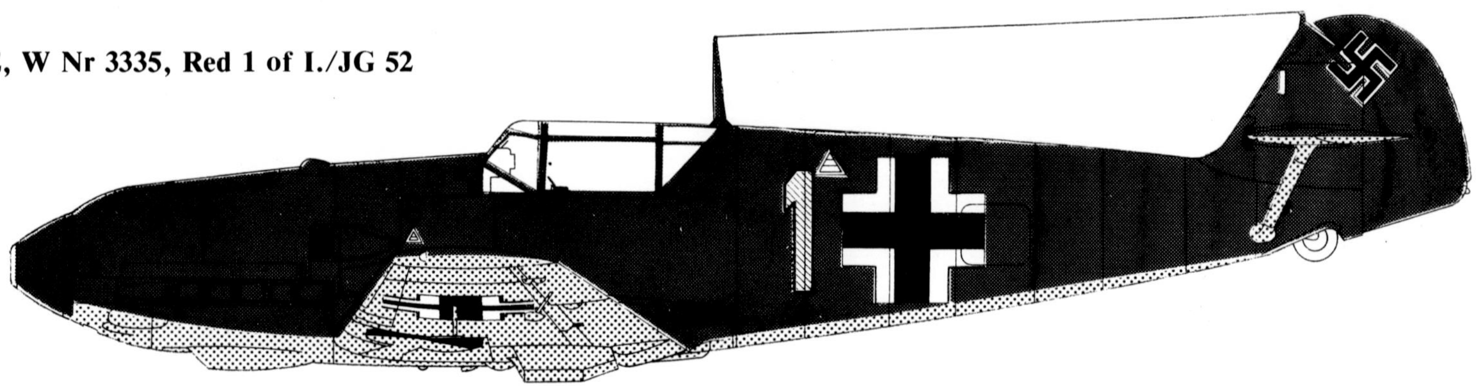

It was in this aircraft that *Lt* Berthel scored JG 52's first victory of the war on 6th October 1939, the victim being a French reconnaissance bomber. The upper surfaces are believed to have been black-green 70 alone, which was most unusual at the time. Its undersurfaces were pale blue 65 with the aircraft's individual number in red. The single victory bar and the *Werk Nummer*, 3335, appeared in white on the rudder although the latter could not be shown on this drawing because it was so small.

Bf 109E, W Nr 5819 of JG 26

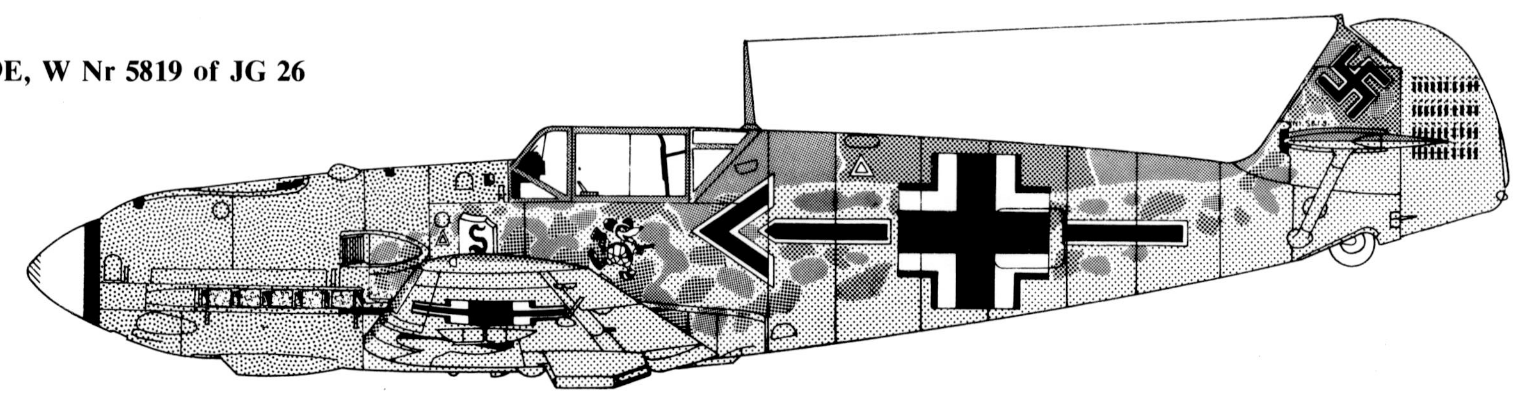

This aircraft with its striking markings belonged to *Maj* Adolf Galland, at the time *Kommodore* of JG 26. It had a grey camouflage scheme with pale blue and 65 undersurfaces and a yellow cowling. The spinner was black, white and red. It carried the JG 26 *Schlageter* emblem in black and white plus a painting of Mickey Mouse as a personel marking. The cockpit frames were painted dark grey, RLM 66. On the rudder were four arrows of ten victories. All victory bars had a circle on top indicating the date of each encounter.

Drawings by R. Sandow

Bf 109E-3, Yellow 15, of I./JG 52

This aircraft was normally flown by *Fw* Kurt Wolff of 3./JG 52. It had an early grey camouflage scheme but its engine cowling, rudder and the upper surfaces of the wingtips were painted an extremely pale washable yellow. The spinner colors were red and white whilst the emblem of I./JG 52 appeared in red, white and blue with the boar shown in black. The special washable markings were used for the anticipated landing and occupation of England during September 1940. It should be noted that a rear vision mirror had been fitted on top of the cockpit canopy.

Bf 109G-2, Yellow 12, of 6./JG 5

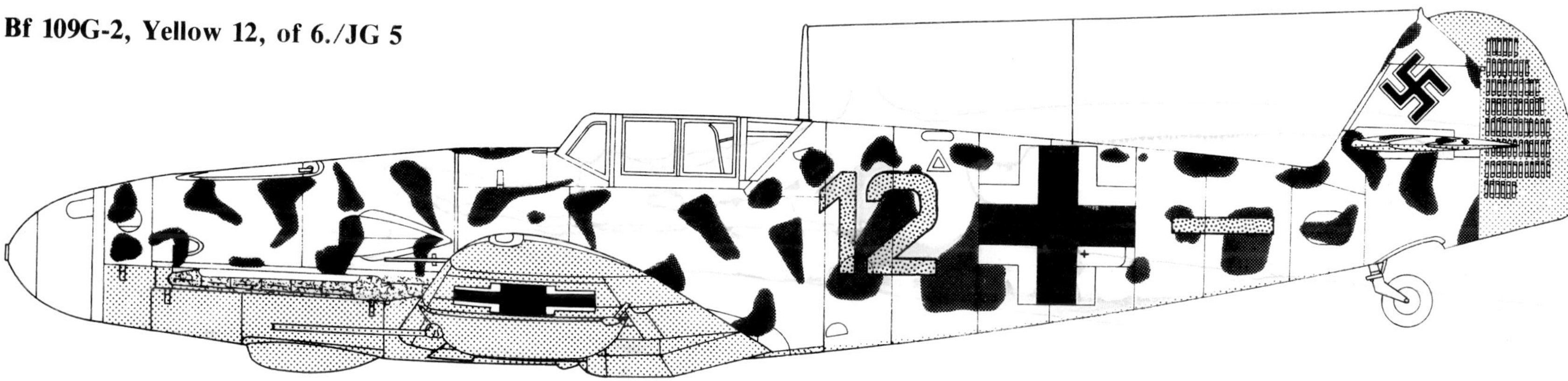

The aircraft shown here belonged to *Oblt* Heinrich Ehrler, *Staffelkapitän* of 6./JG 5. At this time, in March 1943, Ehrler had 77 of his 204 victories shown on his rudder. The rudder itself was probably RLM 76, although a mixture of 76 and 75 would have been quite possible. The upper surfaces of the aircraft were camouflaged in washable white, apparently with RLM 70 patches. The fuselage crosses had also been oversprayed in white. The number 12 and the second *Gruppe* bar were painted in yellow with a thin black border. The undersurfaces were RLM 76. During the summer, this aircraft had the standard grey camouflage scheme. It should be noted that Ehrler at this time sustained a hit in his engine-mounted cannon and the aircraft was replaced, resulting in two aircraft with similar markings.

Drawings by R. Sandow

Bf 109F/Trop, White 12, of 4./JG 27

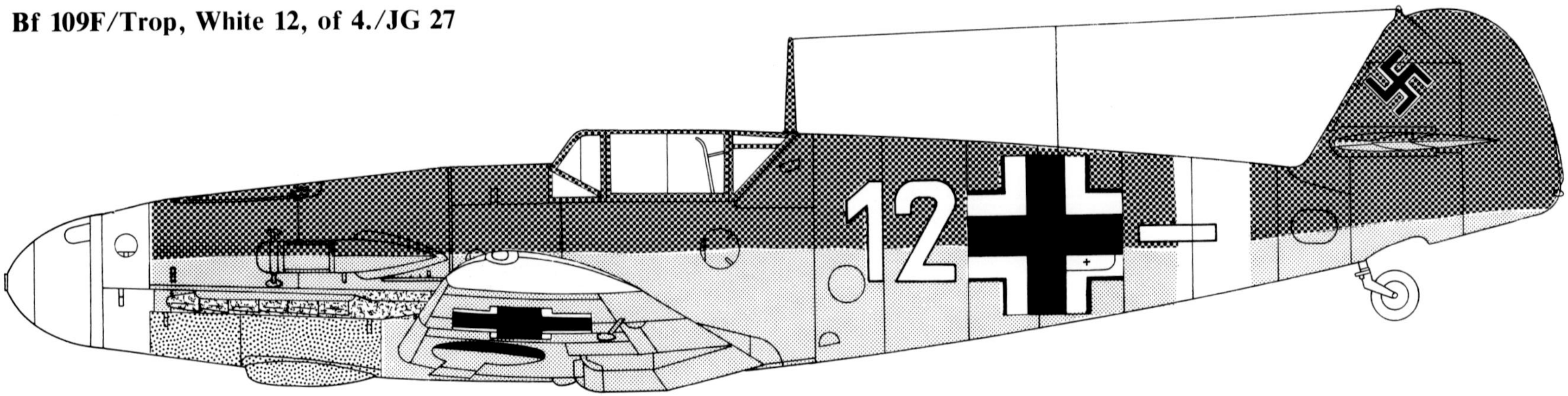

This machine belonged to *Ofw* Franz Stigler. In this case the usual emblem of 4./JG 27, a crash-landing British lion, was not used. The aircraft showed typical tropical camouflage, with upper surfaces in RLM 79 and RLM 78 underneath. The fuselage band, nose, and wingtips were painted in white with the lower part of the engine cowling in yellow.

Bf 109F-2, W Nr 6750 (?) of JG 26

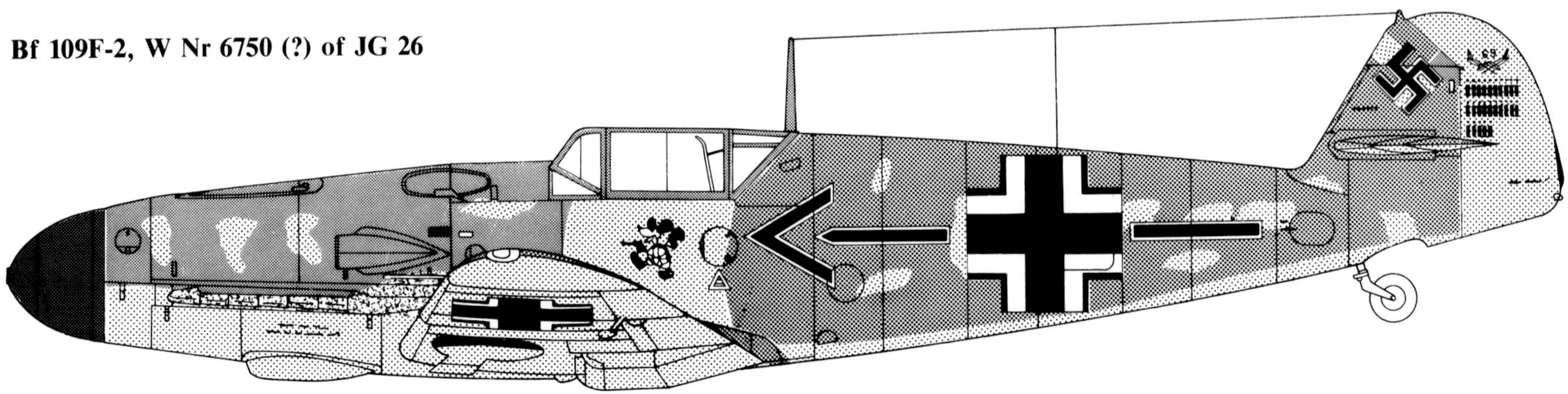

This aircraft, also in *Kommodore* markings, was allocated on *Obst* Adolf Galland of JG 26 during December 1941, before he left to become *Inspekteur der Jagdflieger*. It had had a grey and somewhat indistinct camouflage scheme with the usual black-green 70 spinner. On the rudder was the number 69 in red, surrounded by oak leaves with details in black plus silver swords. There were two further rows of victory bars and a third row with five more victories; a total of 94. All bars appeared in red. The aircraft was equipped with an engine-mounted cannon plus two MG 131s over the engine, the shells being ejected and not collected as on later models. At this time Galland also used a similar aircraft armed with two MG FF guns in the wings plus two MG 17s over the engine.

Bf 109F, W Nr 8693, Yellow 14 of JG 27

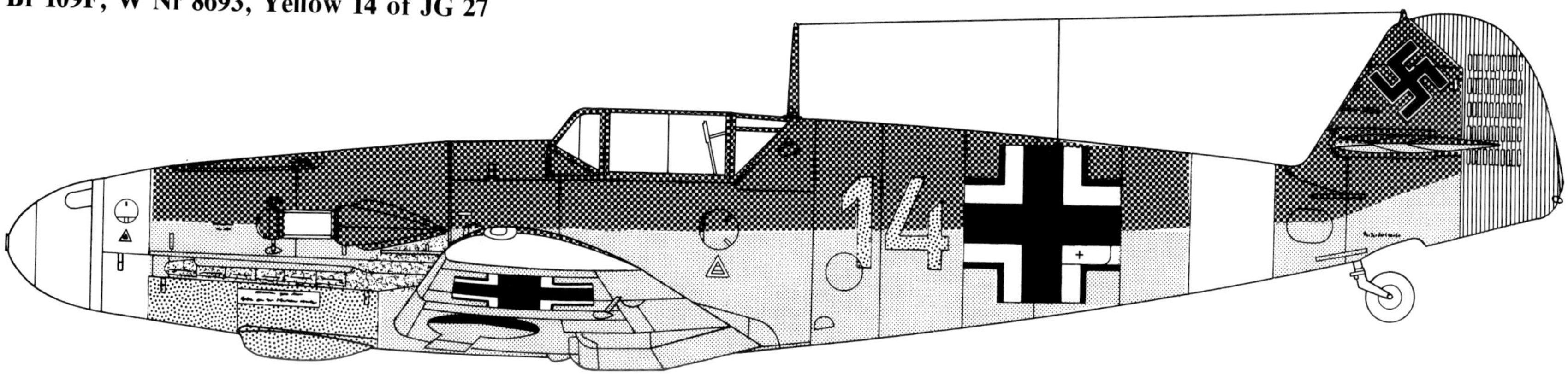

This Messerschmitt was one of the first Bf 109Fs used by the well-known Hans-Joachim Marseille during February 1942. The camouflage was of the standard tropical type with upper surfaces in RLM 79 and with RLM 78 underneath. The spinner, nose, fuselage tail band and undersurfaces of the wingtips were in white. On the reddish-brown primer-colored rudder were 50 victory bars in pale yellow, the same color as the lower engine cowling.

Bf 109F, W Nr 8673, Yellow 14 of JG 27

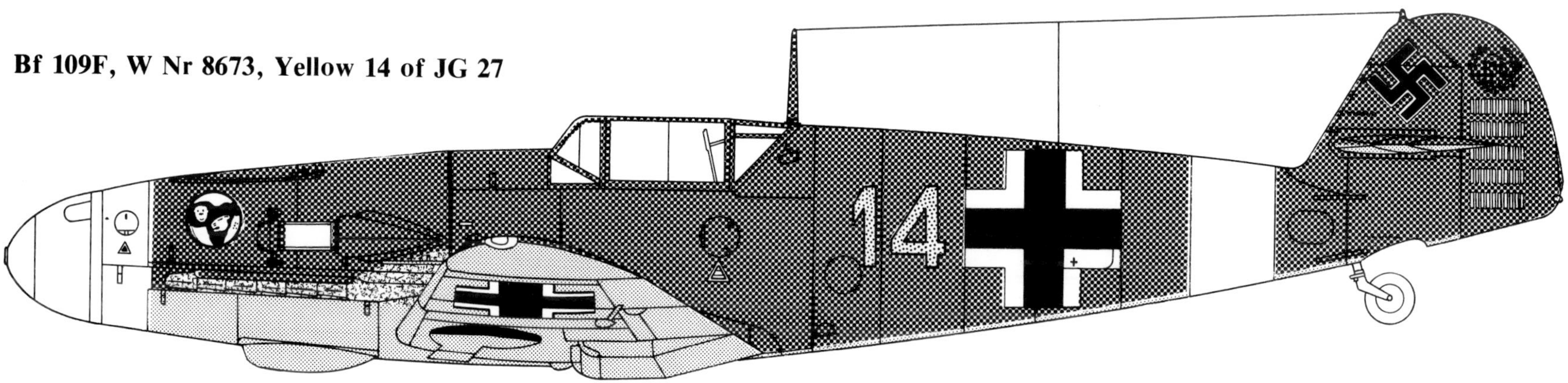

This aircraft was the last Bf 109F used by Marseille before he was killed in September 1942. No information is available about his eight victories in a Bf 109G-2. The camouflage was mainly RLM 79 with RLM 78 underneath. The nose and fuselage tail band were in white, but there were no white wingtips, nor yellow engine cowling. The emblem of I./JG 27, however, appeared on the engine cowling. This was Marseille's only aircraft where the yellow 14 was surrounded by a thin black border. On the rudder was the number 100 surrounded by a wreath of oak leaves, the first row of yellow victory markings having eleven, then four rows with ten each, a total of 151.

Drawings by R. Sandow

Bf 109F, Yellow 7, of 3./JG 51

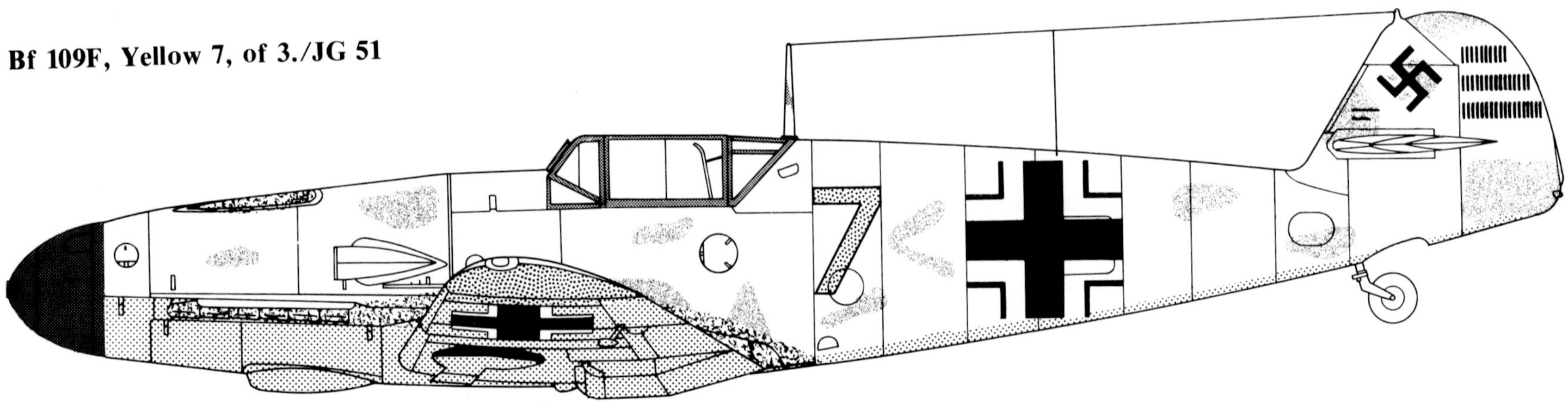

The usual pilot of this aircraft cannot be positively identified, but it may have been *Fw* Erwin Fleig, a very experienced former wingman of Werner Mölders. The upper surfaces were almost totally painted in washable white, but in some places the grey camouflage showed through faintly. The exhausts and gun openings were covered in black grime. The spinner was painted the usual RLM 70, with the lower wingtips in yellow. Yellow 7 had its number surrounded by a black line, but had no customary yellow fuselage band. The undersurfaces were RLM 76. On the rudder were three rows with victories; 10, 15 and 18 respectively, a total of 43, all in black.

Bf 109G-1, Black 13 of 8./JG 52

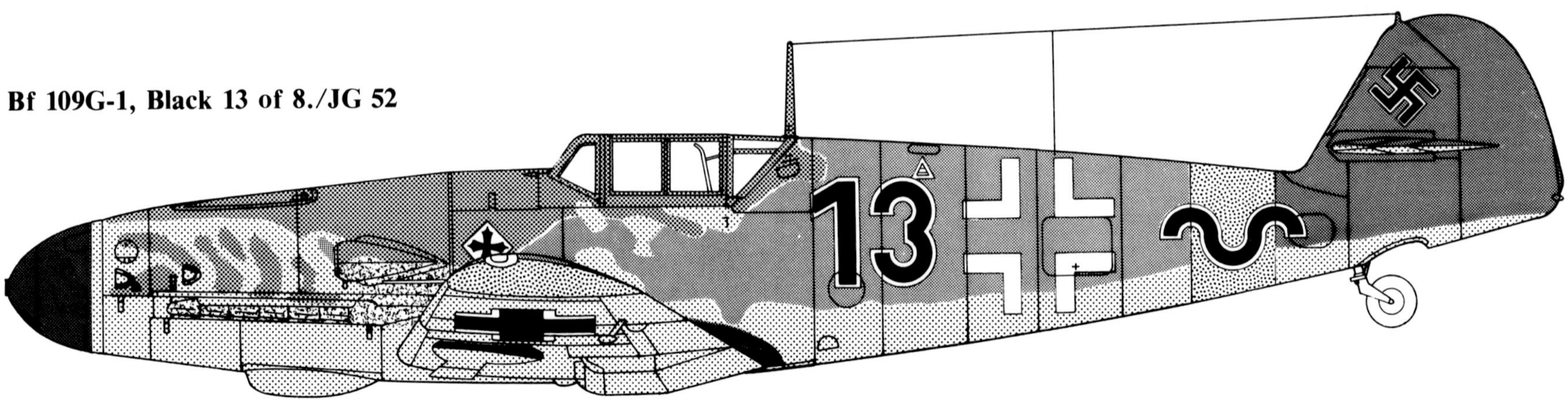

This machine belonged to the notable *Oblt* Günther Rall of 8./JG 52. It had 74/75/76 camouflage consisting of unusually large color areas on top. The number 13 and the *Gruppe* marking were painted in black outlined in white, with the fuselage tail band and lower wingtips in yellow. The spinner was painted the usual black-green 70. The III./JG 52 emblem showed a red cross on a white background surrounded by a thin black border. No victory markings were carried on the rudder and the fuselage section numbers were visible on the lower part of the fuselage sides.

Fw 190A-5/U-12, Red 13, W Nr 410266 of 2./JG 11

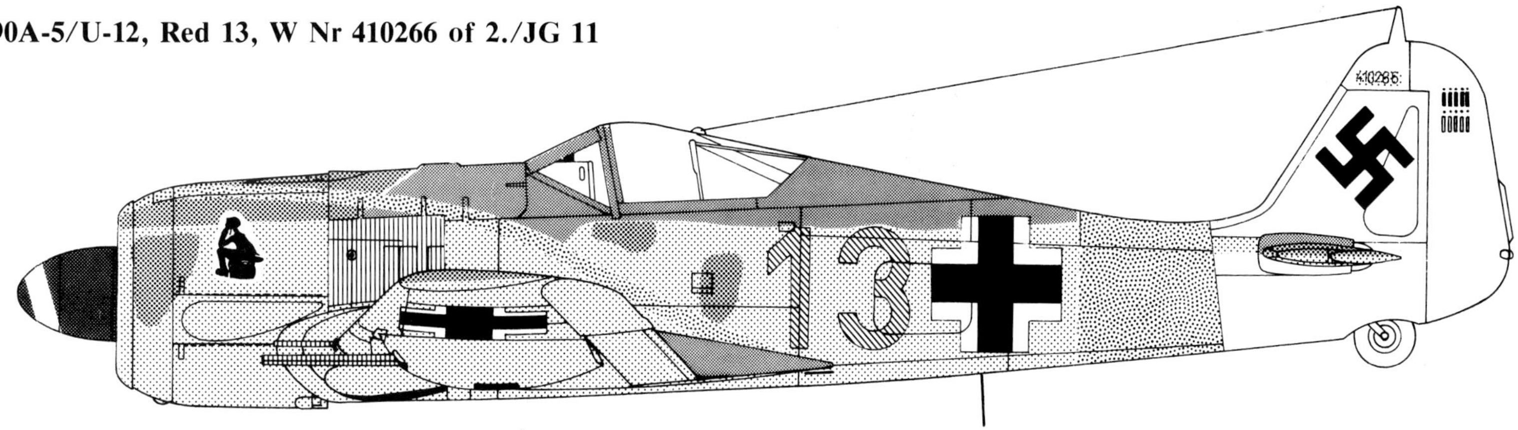

Drawings by R. Sandow

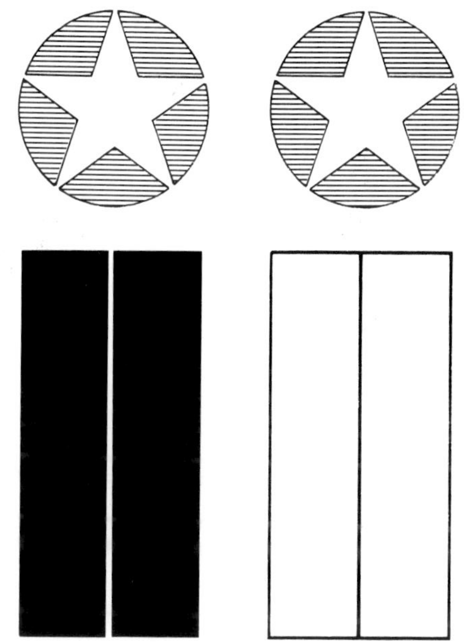

This aircraft was flown by *Lt* Erich Hondt, *Staffelkapitän* of 2./JG 11 during 1943. Although the normal grey camouflage scheme was used, the machine was still very colorful. It was coded Red 13 with the fuselage tailband in yellow and a completely white rudder showing a grey area around the *Werk Nummer* and ten victories over American aircraft. (See detail drawing). The spinner was painted RLM 70, with possibly one segment in yellow plus a white spiral. A yellow line swept from the nose on each side, whilst the engine cowling bore the hitherto unknown emblem of 8./JG 11. The lower drawings show the basically black and white emblem of 8./JG 11, the rear part of the man's hat being either brown or red. The victory bars in the upper row were shown in black with the lower row in white plus a thin black outline. The American markings were blue and white.

Drawings by R. Sandow

Bf 109G-5/R6, Red 3, W Nr 15912 of JGr 50

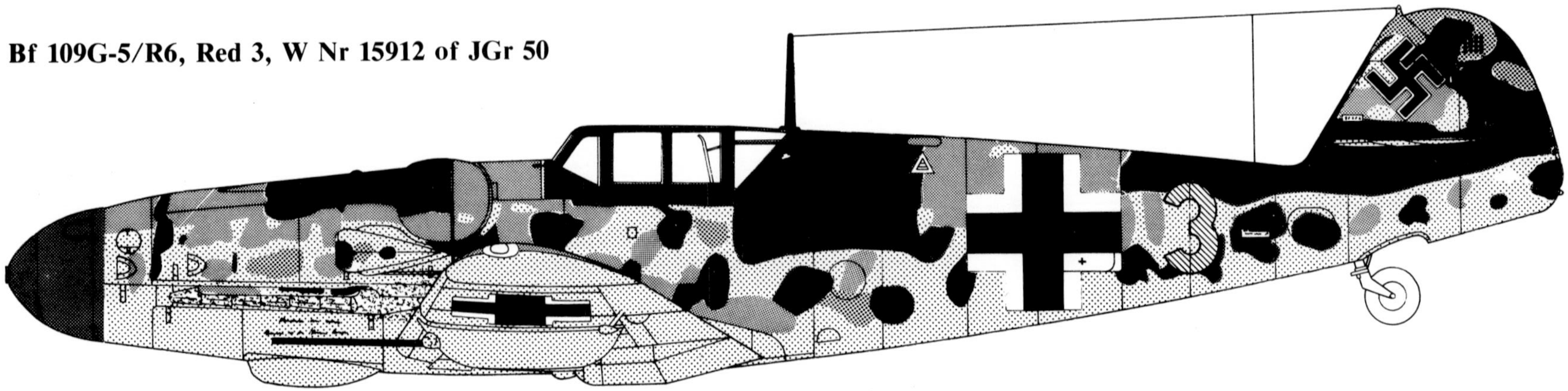

Published a number of times but never positively identified, this was the aircraft of *Lt* Gottfried Weiroster of JGr 50, a unit led by Herrmann Graf. Red 3 had basic grey 75 camouflage with heavy use of RLM 70. It also had a high-gloss surface to help increase the machine's top speed. On the rudder were four black victory markings, one of them including an American star. The red number 3 was surrounded by a white line. On this aircraft all stencilling had been left completely exposed rather than covered by camouflage as was very common.

Bf 109G-6, Yellow 1, W Nr 20499 of 9./JG 52

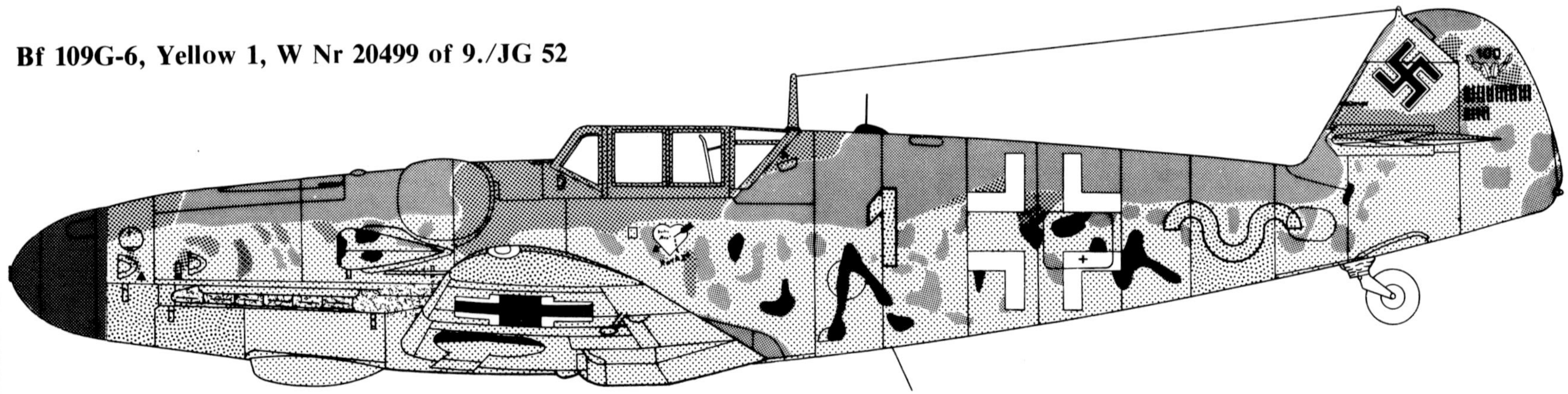

This aircraft belonged to the *Staffelkapitän* of 9./JG 52, the very successful *Lt* Erich Hartmann. Its camouflage was 74/75/76 with small areas of RLM 70 on the fuselage sides. The lower cowling, wingtips number 1, the III. *Gruppe* marking and the fuselage tail band were all in yellow. On the rudder was a century marking outlined thinly in black. The oak leaves were in green, with black details. In addition there were 21 victory bars in red. The pilot's personal red heart marking had a yellow arrow with yellow drops and the name *Karaya*, also in yellow. Written on the heart in white was the inscription *Dicker Max* (Big Show). About one sixth of the black-green 70 spinner was segmented in white.

Bf 109G-5/R6, Red 1, W Nr 15913 of JGr 50

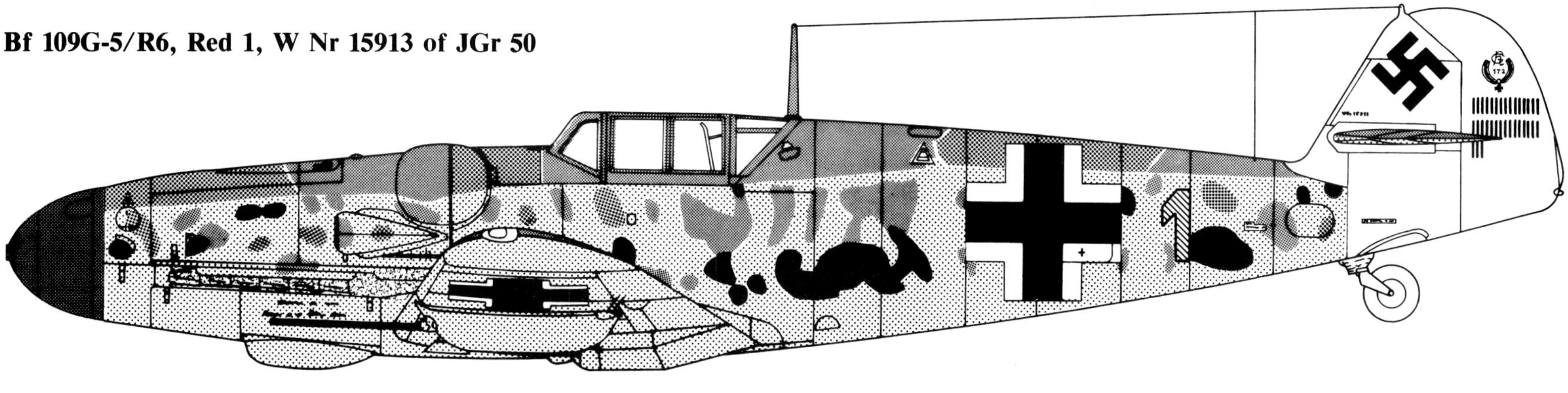

Hermann Graf flew this machine as *Kommandeur* of JGr 50, a unit based at Wiesbaden-Erbenheim, flying sorties against high-flying Allied aircraft. Red 1 had standard grey camouflage with black-green 70 patches and spinner. On a completely white rudder were Graf's personal markings; a 172-victory emblem, then two rows with 15 victories, each recording Russian aircraft, plus three victories over American aircraft. His *Gustav* is depicted as at 6th September 1943.

FW 190A-7/R2, Black 1, W Nr 07169 (?) of JG 11

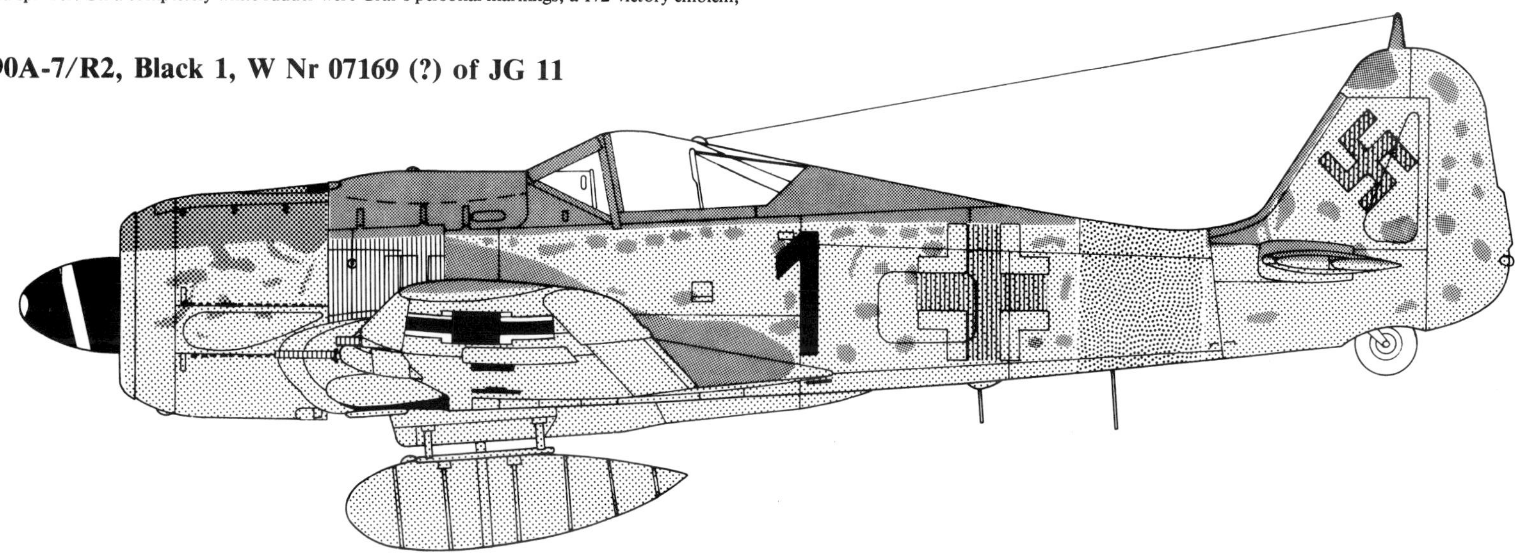

This machine was flown by the *Staffelkapitän* of 2./JG 11 during February 1944. Its pilot cannot be positively identified but it was either *Lt* Alwin Doppler of *Ritterkreuzträger* Josef Zwernemann. It had a grey camouflage scheme with an oversprayed fuselage cross and swastika, a black number 1 and a black spinner with encircling white spiral. The yellow fuselage tail band indicated JG 11. The area around the cooling flaps was the usual grimy black and the aircraft was equipped with 30-mm MK 108 cannon in the outboard sections of the wings. Overspraying of the markings made the aircraft extremely difficult to detect at low altitude, this ruse being widely used by JG 11 during 1944.

Drawings by R. Sandow

Bf 109G-6 with dual chevron, of I./JG 52

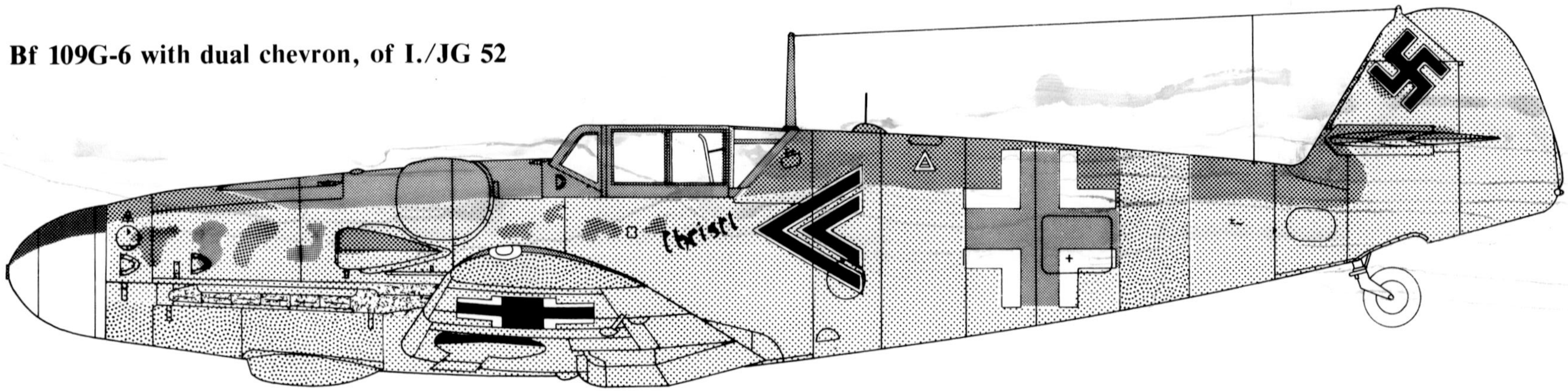

During the late summer of 1943 this aircraft was extensively used by the *Gruppenkommandeur* of I./JG 52, *Hpt* Gerhard Barkhorn. Its standard grey camouflage scheme had a semi-matt, rather silken appearance. It displayed the usual yellow fuselage tailband, lower wingtips and engine cowling. Its spinner was mainly white with approximately one third being painted black-green 70. Under the cockpit was his wife's name, Christl, which appeared in white and which was similar to that already published of his Bf 109G-5 or G-6 of II./JG 52. No victory bars nor unit emblem appeared on this machine.

Bf 109G-6AS with dual chevron, of II./JG 11

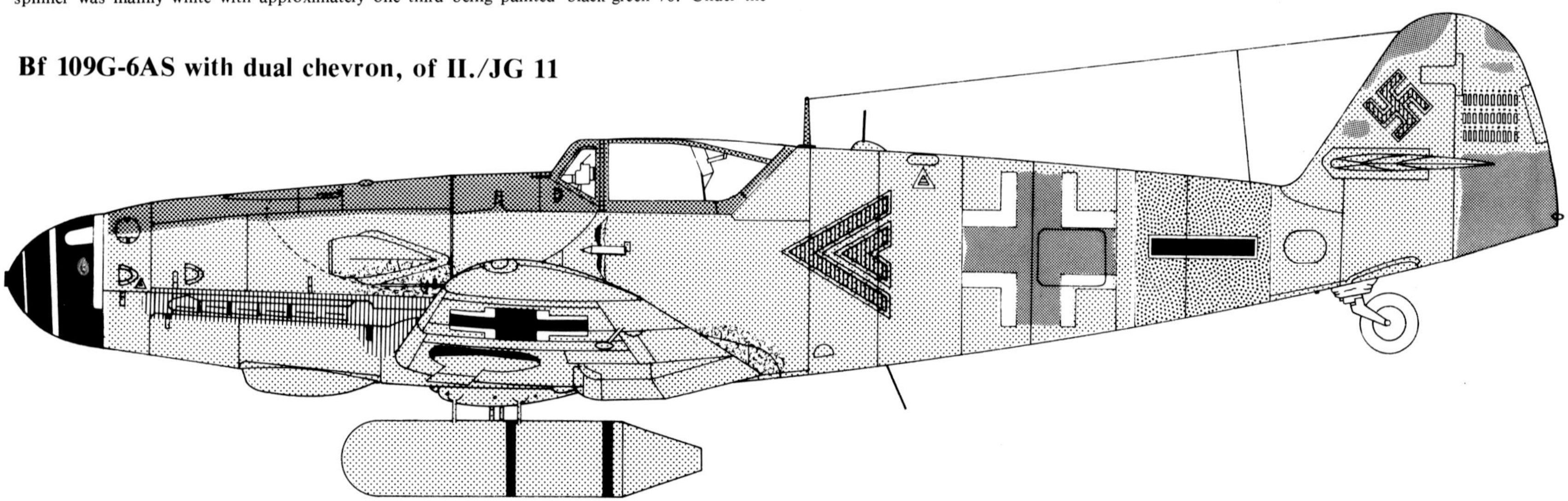

During April 1944 this aircraft was flown by the unit's *Gruppenkommandeur*, *Maj* Günther Specht. It had a very different 74/75/76 camouflage scheme with much overspraying, so that swastika and chevrons, including the white border lines, appeared as grey shades. Around the exhaust pipes was a black-painted area, followed by much discoloration. On the black spinner was a rather crudely applied white spiral. The rudder showed three rows of ten victories each. Above the first six bars were British roundels whilst above the others American stars were shown. Within each victory bar the aircraft type was indicated, the lower section showing the date of the victory. Under the cockpit was Specht's personal emblem, a winged pencil. Its colors were three shades of brown with wings in black, white and grey. The machine is shown here with a slightly unusual type of long-range fuel tank.

Me 262A-1, White 9, W Nr 111617 of E JG 2

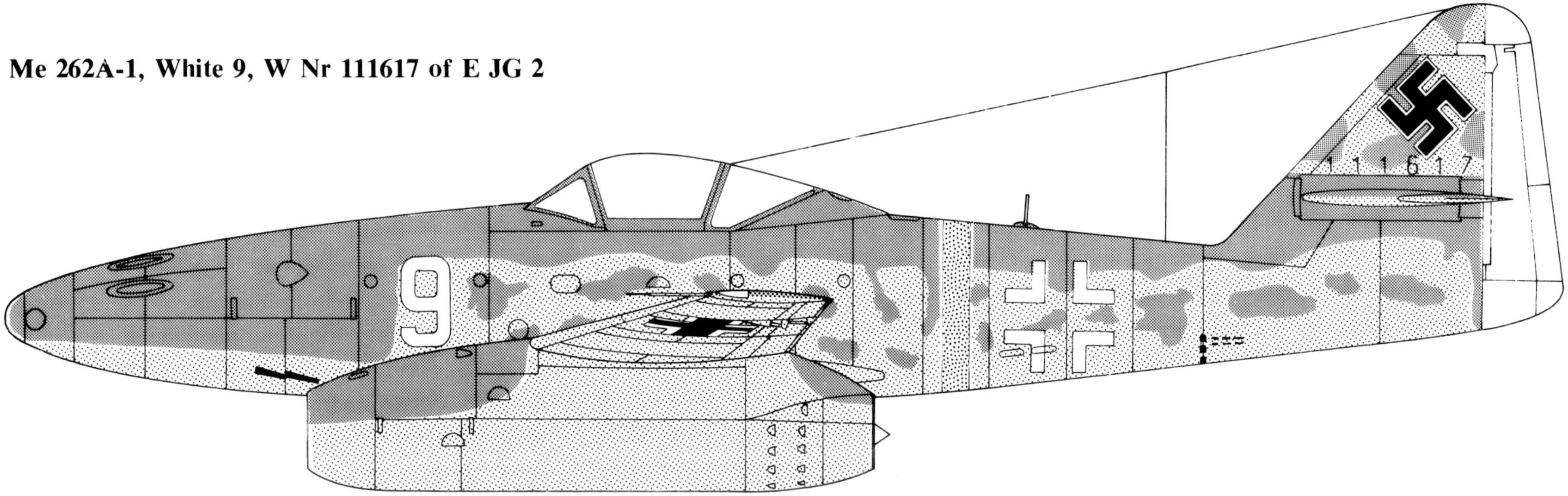

This aircraft was usually flown by *Fjofw* Recker of *Ergänzungsjagdgeschwader* 2. It was an example of the early grey scheme with RLM 74 alone on the upper surfaces and RLM 76 underneath. On the fuselage it bore a white number 9 with a yellow tail band whilst at the rear of each engine a thin red ring had been painted. The rudder was a very light color, either a dirty white or an extremely light shade of pale blue-grey 76, by no means an uncommon feature of fighter camouflage of the period.

He 162A-2, Yellow 5, W Nr ? of JG 1

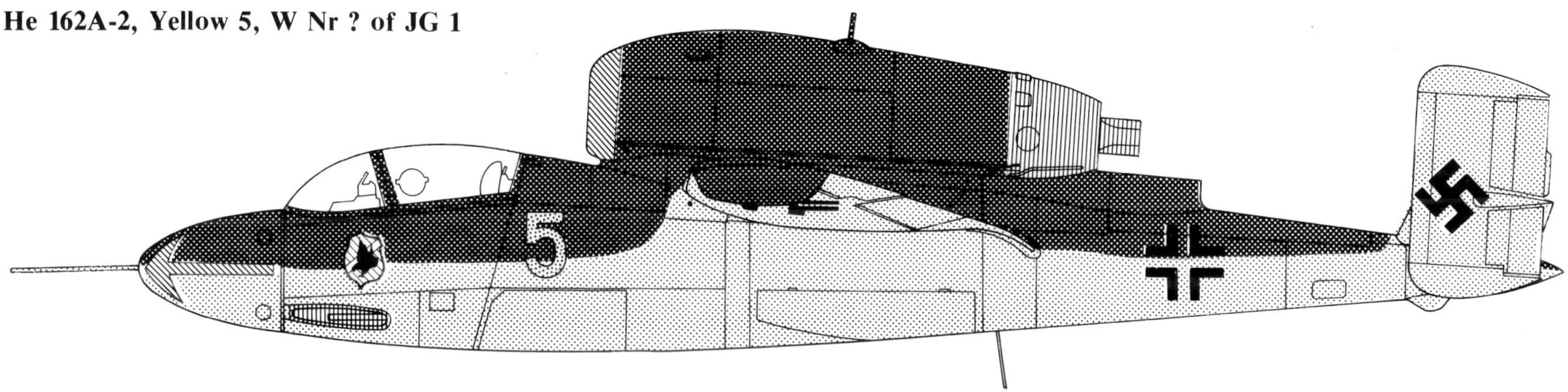

This aircraft was actually flown operationally by *Hpt* Heinz Künnecke of I./JG 1. The upper surfaces were probably either dark green 71 or 82 with pale blue-grey 76 underneath. The fuselage crosses and swastikas were shown in black. The black *Werk Nummer* is not known, but was probably also in the 120… series. The striking arrows on the nose and the engine intake were in red, with the rear end of the engine and the cannon openings in black. The number 5 appeared in yellow with a thin black border. The emblem had a red and white background whilst the eagle itself was black with yellow details, the whole being surrounded by a thin black border.

Drawings by R. Sandow

He 162A-2, White 11, W Nr 120074 of JG 1

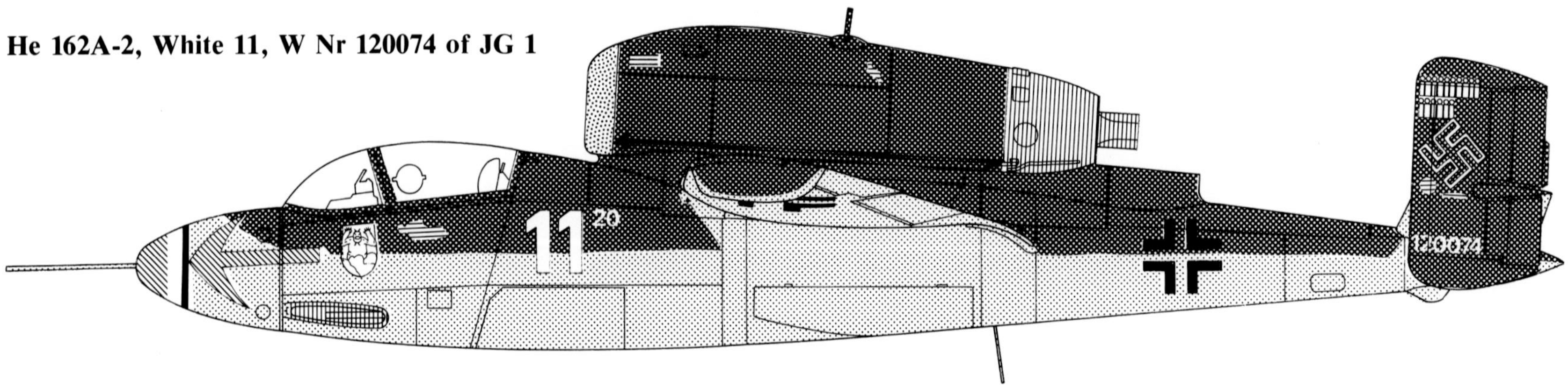

This particular Heinkel was flown by the *Gruppenkommandeur* of I./JG 1, *Oblt* Karl Demuth. Its upper surfaces were probably also dark green 71 or 82 with pale blue-grey 76 underneath. The fuselage crosses were in black whilst on the dark rudder the swastikas and 16 American victories appeared in white. The engine intake was yellow with the rear end in black. The nose of this aircraft was red, white and black with red arrows. The emblem of I./JG 1 had a yellow background with white clouds whilst the devil was a flesh color with details in black. The gun apertures were also in black. Eleven was the pilot's favorite number, the small 20 here indicating the unit's *Gruppenkommandeur*.

Me 262A-1, Red 3 and chevron, of JG 7

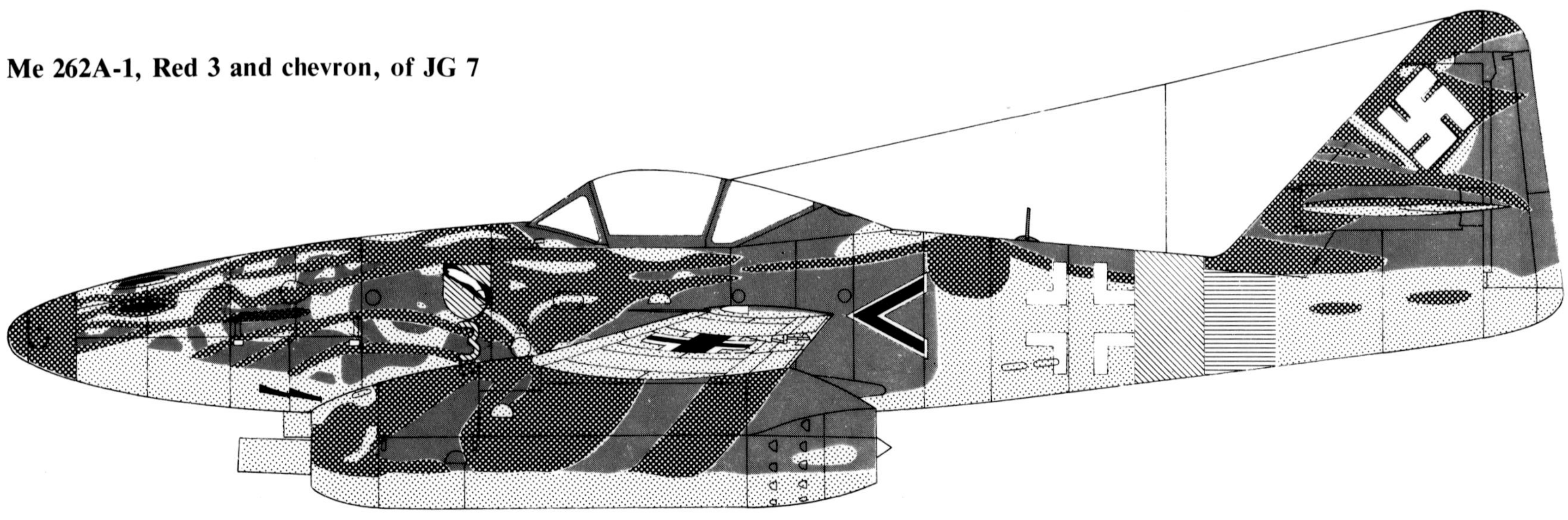

The usual pilot of this machine cannot be positively identified, but the aircraft is believed to have been flown at one time by *Maj* Rudi Sinner, *Kommandeur* of III./JG 7 during 1945. It had a camouflage scheme consisting of long brownish-green 81 streaks over dark green 82 with pale blue-grey 76 underneath. The nose cone was brownish-green 81. The fuselage crosses were in white with the tail band shown in red and blue with the red leading. The chevrons were black with white borders, the unusual swastikas being all-white. Just forward of the cockpit was the emblem of JG 7 in blue, red and white whilst underneath was a red number 3 with a white border. The aircraft was equipped with two BR 21 rocket launching tubes fitted to the lower fuselage.

Color Section

These two informal shots were taken when JG 52 was operating on the Eastern Front in 1943. The photo above shows the unit's doctor, and behind him a Bf 109G-6 "Black 3." Below: Gerhard Barkhorn (left) *Gruppenkommandeur* II./JG 52, chats with *Lt* Plücker at Charkow-Rogan in Russia. Although Barkhorn had won the *Eichenlaub* for 120 victories by this time, he wears no decorations.

Messerschmitt Bf 109F-2

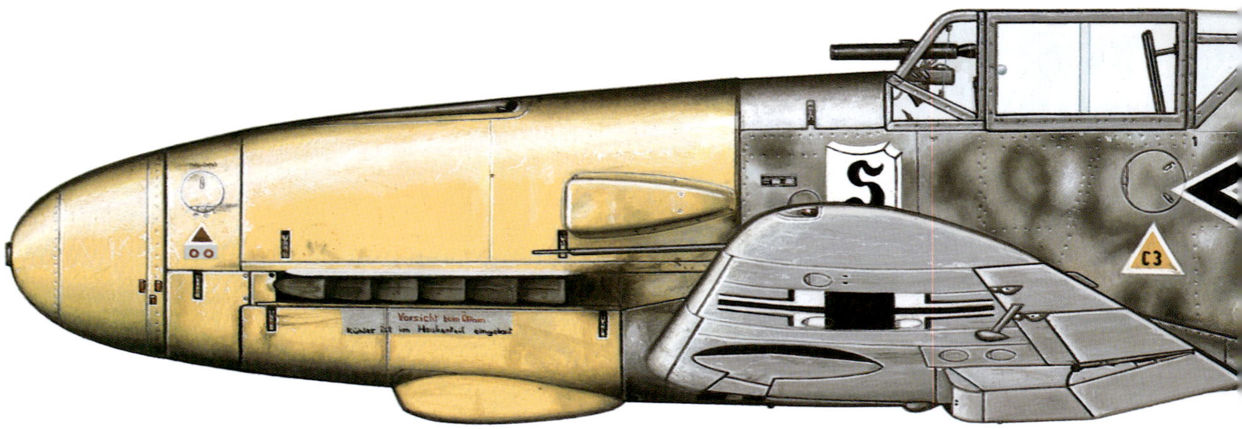

W Nr 6714, of JG 26

The camouflage scheme was an early grey one, and it is not clea used at this time were the official RLM 74/75/76 or not. The en rudder were in pale yellow, with the victory bars in red except for black, a total of 60.

The markings were those of a *Kommodore*, with the *Schlaget* JG 26, but Galland's personal Mickey Mouse badge was not carri of the machine were painted symmetrically. As a special featur was fitted with a ZFR 5 telescopic sight, but Galland only used

Adolf Galland

Painting by Richard Goyat

range identification, not for aiming. During this period, in April 1941, the Staff element of JG 26 was based at Brest-Guipavas in North-western France.

As a *Major*, Galland had been awarded the *Eichenlaub* during September 1940 for 40 victories. As an *Oberstleutnant* he was to receive the *Schwerter* (Swords) on 21st June 1941 for 69 victories. Second only to Mölders, and as an *Oberst*, he was awarded the *Brillanten* (Diamonds) on 28th January 1942, for his 94 victories.

Messerschmitt Bf 109F-4/Tr

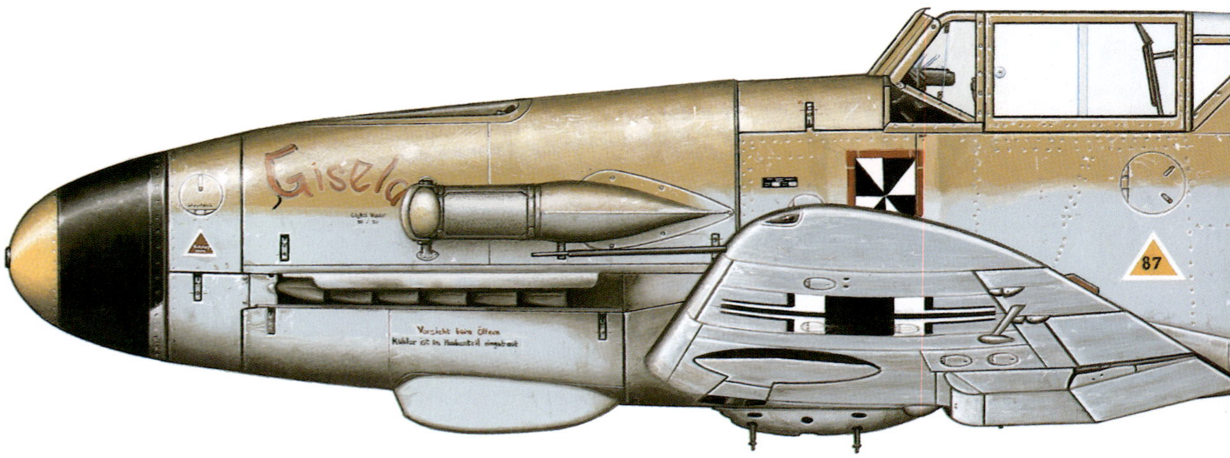

JG 3, February 1942

This aircraft displayed a typical tropical camouflage scheme, w surfaces in RLM 79 and RLM 78 underneath. The badge of II. black and white with a red border. The yellow 3 and the bar *Gruppe* was outlined in black. On the cowling was the name Gise black details, after the pilot's girlfriend at that time.

In this aircraft of 6./JG 3, Schwaiger took off his 120th operati 23rd February 1942, to fly from Pantelleria to Castel Benito in

Franz Schwaiger

Painting by Richard Goyat

At this time he had eight victories. On 29th October 1942, as an *Unteroffizier*, he was awarded the *Ritterkreuz* for 52 victories in the East.

On 24th April 1944, having 67 victories including 12 in the West, he made an emergency landing due to lack of fuel at Pessenburgheim after destroying an American four-engined bomber in his Bf 109G, White 15. An American fighter pilot witnessed this and killed Schwaiger after he had left his aircraft. He was *Staffelkapitän* of 1./JG 3 at the time.

Focke-Wulf Fw 190A-5

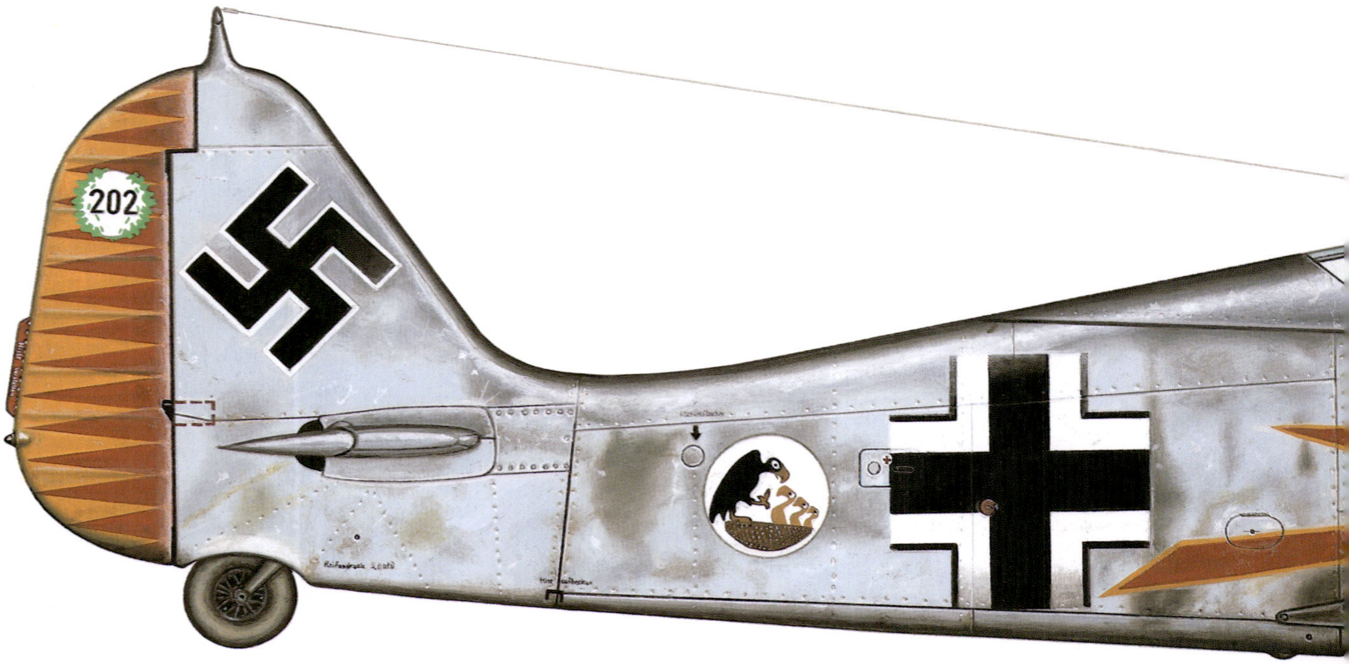

W Nr 2594, of *Jagd Erg Gr Ost*

This aircraft was probably one of the most colorful ever
Luftwaffe. The marking of Hermann Graf (202 victories) is the hig
documented by photographs. The aircraft camouflage colors wer
and 76. The cowling was deep yellow with red triangles, separa
white line. The front armor ring was in white and the spinner, gl
The red and yellow rudder showed a white circle surrounded
leaves, with the number 202 shown in black. In front of the fusela

Hermann Graf

Painting by Richard Goyat

red flash outlined in yellow and behind it the bird's-nest emblem of a *Jagdergänzungsgruppe*, probably *Jagdergänzungsgruppe Ost*, commanded in France by Graf during 1943.

Graf flew several different aircraft, this one being equipped with a modified two-stage supercharger and special intakes, as shown. He was the first pilot to gain 200 victories, reaching 202 on 2nd October 1942. His total claim was 212, 202 in the East, and ten four-engined bombers in the West.

Messerschmitt Bf 109G-5/R

JG 11, early 1944

This aircraft was finished in the standard grey camouflage scheme. The upper surface was in RLM 74 and 75 over RLM 76, the base coat underneath. The yellow fuselage band was the home defence marking for JG 11. The double chevron, the *Balkenkreuz* and the bar of the third *Gruppe* were in black and white, with the spinner in white and RLM 70.

The white rudder displayed the *Ritterkreuz* with *Eichenlaub* with the red 100 surrounded by a wreath of green oak leaves. The 32 victory bars were in black. This aircraft was fitted with a 300-litre drop tank and MG 151/20 underwing

Anton Hackl

Painting by Richard Goyat

gondolas.

The aircraft carried the markings of a *Gruppenkommandeur* of III./JG 11 and was used by Anton Hackl at the beginning of 1944 in addition to a similarly marked Fw 190. He received the *Eichenlaub* for 104 victories on 6th August 1942. With a total of 192 victories plus a further 24 unconfirmed (87 in the West, including 32 four-engined bombers) during over a thousand missions, he was one of the most successful of all German fighter pilots.

Heinkel He 162A-2

W Nr 120027, of JG 1

The camouflage on this aircraft was RLM 71 and RLM 76, the red arrow being merely an embellishment. The diving eagle badge was probably that of 1./JG 1, but this cannot be verified. On this He 162 the number 120027 is provisional, for neither the pilot's log book nor the rudder photo could provide the actual number. On the rudder shot, due to the high gloss finish, only the first three digits, indicating Rostock-Marienehe production, could be discerned.

W Nr 120027 was chosen because White 3 (W Nr 120028) and a crashed aircraft (W Nr 120029) both had very similar camouflage. It should be noted that

Rudolf Schmitt

Painting by Richard Goyat

the camouflage of He 162s differed from aircraft to aircraft. Light-colored fins and rudders were also used.

The fuselage *Balkenkreuz* had obviously been applied in some haste. White 1 was one Heinkel which saw genuine action and the *Staffelkapitän* of 1./JG 1, *Lt* Rudolf Schmitt, claimed one of the unit's few victories, a Typhoon, with this machine on 24th April 1945. Due to the chaotic war situation this claim was never confirmed officially.

Messerschmitt Bf 109G-14 A

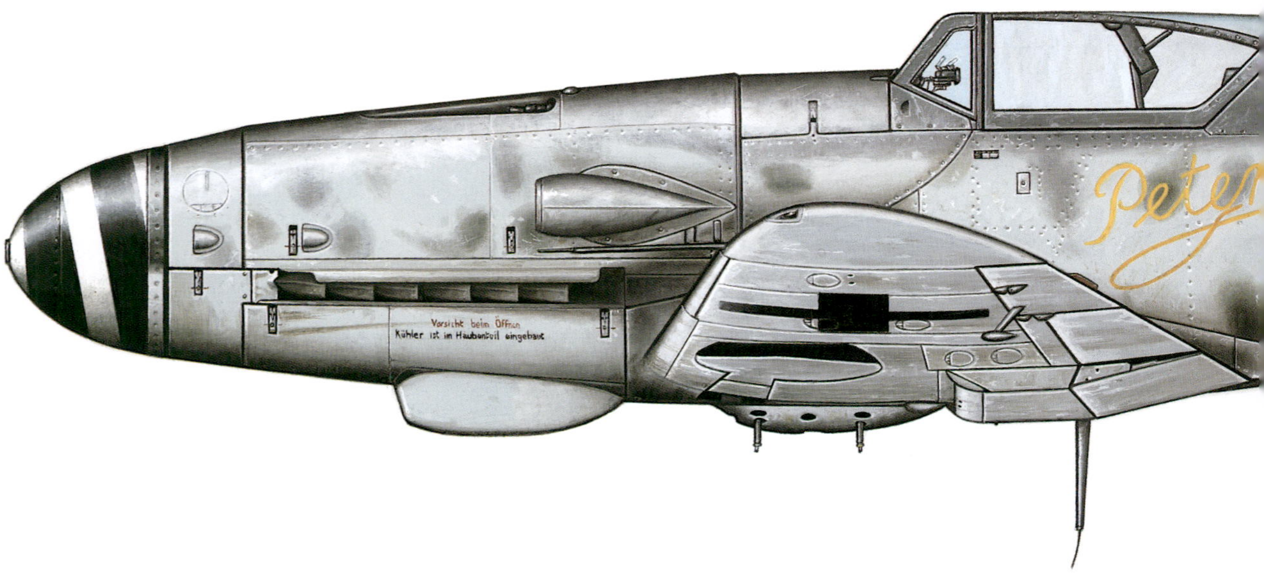

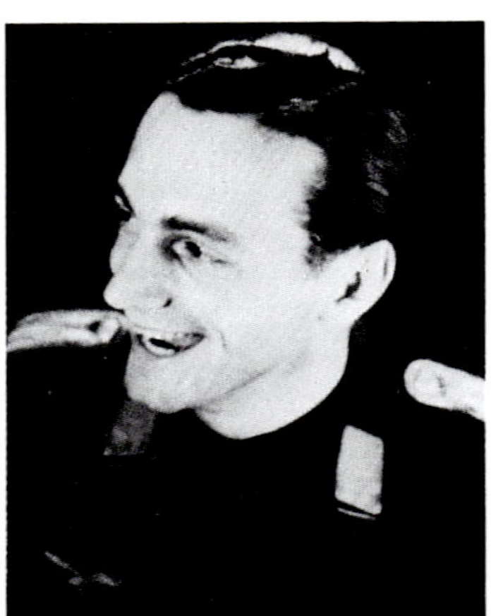

JG 4, late 1944

This late-model Bf 109 with the refined cowling showed a m
74/75/76 camouflage with spots of RLM 74/02 and also 70 or
sides. It belonged to the *Staffelkapitän* of 14./JG 4, *Oblt* Err
Black 13 displayed the home defence tail band of JG 4 (black,
combined with the IV. *Gruppe* marking. At this time, about A
Scheufele had a girlfriend nicknamed *Peterle*, from the song of th
This name was also painted in yellow on the left side of the coc

Ernst Scheufele

Painting by Richard Goyat

Ernst Scheufele at first flew cover for the navy, but he later joined II./JG 5 and served in the East; then to IV./JG 4 flying on home defence duties under *Kommodore* Michalski. On 3rd December 1944 he was shot down by ground-fire from an American supply unit near Aachen. He had a total of 18 victories, including three four-engined bombers and two P-51 Mustangs. Two of his claims were unconfirmed.

Johannes Wiese (right) with comrades in front of a Bf 109E of E/JG 52 at Elbing.

Two Bf 109Gs of JG 52, "White 5" (above), and "White 10" (below) being serviced somewhere on the Eastern Front.

Two shots of Walter Horten of III./JG 26 in the cockpit of his Bf 109E, "White 7." Note the faded condition of the temporary yellow paint on the forward part of the cowling.

Above is an interesting shot of *Oblt* Herman Segatz *Staffelkapitän* of 8./JG 5. His aircraft displays the Tyrolean eagle emblem.

Seen here is Walter Horten, *Gruppenkommandeur* of III./JG 26, in front of his Bf 109E. The aircraft has a camouflage scheme consisting of 71/02/65 with some lower areas repainted. Note the auxiliary fuel tank.

These two photos show the crude conditions for maintenance on the Eastern Front, 1943. The aircraft shown is a Bf 109G-6 of JG 52.

Pilots of I/JG 3 Udet at a pre-flight meeting on the Channel front. Bf 109Es in the background with yellow cowlings and wing tips.